Education Game Changers

Education Game Changers

Leadership and the Consequence of Policy Paradox

Karen E. Starr

ROWMAN & LITTLEFIELD
Lanham • Boulder • New York • London

Published by Rowman & Littlefield
A wholly owned subsidiary of The Rowman & Littlefield Publishing Group, Inc.
4501 Forbes Boulevard, Suite 200, Lanham, Maryland 20706
www.rowman.com

Unit A, Whitacre Mews, 26-34 Stannery Street, London SE11 4AB

Copyright © 2015 by Karen E. Starr

All rights reserved. No part of this book may be reproduced in any form or by any electronic or mechanical means, including information storage and retrieval systems, without written permission from the publisher, except by a reviewer who may quote passages in a review.

British Library Cataloguing in Publication Information Available

Library of Congress Cataloging-in-Publication Data

Library of Congress Cataloging-in-Publication Data Available
ISBN 978-1-4758-0631-1 (cloth : alk. paper) -- ISBN 978-1-4758-0632-8 (pbk. : alk. paper) -- ISBN 978-1-4758-0633-5 (electronic)

Contents

Preface   vii
Acknowledgments   xi

1. Change, Challenge, and Paradox   1
2. Economic Constraint versus Social Imperative   11
3. Equity versus Excellence   27
4. Efficiency versus Productivity   41
5. Autonomy versus Control   49
6. Individual Differentiation versus Standardization   63
7. "New World" versus "Old World" Thinking   77
8. Sustainability versus Growth   89
9. Work-Life Balance versus Work Intensification   97
10. The Genie Is Out of the Bottle: Game-Changing Paradox, Dissonance and Dissent   109

References   117

Preface

Boston, Massachusetts, is a most appropriate place to be writing the preface to this book. Renowned as an education heartland, this beautiful city is home to over fifty universities, including the elite institutions Harvard and MIT, with the grand Boston Public Library, "Built by the People and Dedicated to the Advancement of Learning," boasting pride of place in Copley Square.

Since my arriving from Melbourne, Australia, education has been front-page news—local and national, with good, bad, and shocking headlines—a testament to how far-reaching, attention grabbing, and diverse stories about education can be. Everyone has a personal interest or investment in education and, usually, virulent and burly opinions about it.

Topics of news reports are wide-ranging: improved annual standardized test scores, graduation, and truancy rates in some states and declines in others; moves to de-stigmatize free school meals for students in need; elementary and secondary school students taking online courses in virtual universities; a student's high court challenge against a school suspension; felony charges filed against two schoolgirls for cyber-bullying leading to a classmate's suicide; the murders of two teachers; the aftermath of a school massacre one year later.

Concurrently, in Boston's mayoral contest—the first in twenty-two years—education tops the political agendas of the major contenders. All of this is in one day's news—alongside countless television commercials for educational institutions touting their school for enrollments.

These headlines say a lot about, and feed into, the contested arena of education policy. At the heart of the headlines are policy debates about educational standards, education equity, advantage and disadvantage, the cost associated with education at every level, the risks to be mitigated by educational leaders, including fresh problems arising from new technologies, and endless concerns about education "crises." The contents of this book tap into these well-established, perennial debates about education policy—the "stuff" that shapes and becomes the education system we have, the education we experience, the nature of educational work, and the issues with which educational leaders must contend.

This book was born of personal interest and emerged out of professional disquiet about many education policy developments. As an educator, it intersects personal values and lived experience, scholarly interest and the academic requirement to conduct research and publish, as well as professional theorizing and praxis.

Morphologically it connects the personal and the political, the social and cultural. As the following chapters reveal, these concerns are shared. The interviews, observations, and literature reviews conducted for the research disclose a range of contentious common themes and issues confronting educators, particularly those charged with leading, managing, and governing educational institutions. Many problems stem from a mismatch between the values commonly upheld by educators and those that have arrived on the tide of globalization.

The policy paradoxes chronicled in this book are constantly evolving and transforming, and cover a growing range of game-changing phenomena, while having enormous effects. They will change education, as we currently know it, irrevocably.

This book provided an opportunity for "situated theorizing" (Fraser, 1989), and my peers in education—in the schooling, higher education, and training sectors—have been willing to corroborate by expressing their views and describing their experiences. The research combines empirical and critical analyses of complex issues and activities and their existential consequences. It is a response to problems that originated in political practice, which in turn provides the only means by which responses can be created.

The impetus to write this book emerged from concerns about contradictory pressures at play across a range of education policy areas, with remarkable similarities occurring across the developed world. Education policies and an extraordinary array of commentaries supporting, opposing, or ambivalent to them, intersect to form contradictions and antagonisms.

These positions reflect the current state of policy flux with confusion, overlaps, and elisions evidenced in education policy, especially in the context of the massive changes pervading society in general. The research found remarkable agreement among respondents, making the undertaking of this study even more tantalizing and appealing.

Such contradictions and confusion raise many questions and challenges about the future of education, including policy, provision, modes of delivery, equity, curriculum, pedagogy and instruction, teacher education, learning and learners, "quality" and "standards," accountability, educational leadership, and business and governance.

Researching this book suggested that there is very little clarity, let alone agreement, about current policy trends and their implications. Those who work in the field admit to being perplexed as to how these policies, the paradox and confusion they highlight or the developments they spawn, might play out in the longer term. Practitioners and policy makers concur, however, that globalization and international education policy developments are creating an inundation of change.

Underscored are the contradictions created through the principles and values inherent in global free-market economic imperatives and their corresponding neoliberal policy narratives being employed in a social realm such as education. Applied in an international context, there will be many similar problems to address and goals to achieve, infused with diverse and nuanced local interpretations and responses, albeit with stalwarts of benchmarking and "learning from the best" attempting to emulate top achievers irrespective of contextual differences.

Education Game-Changers reviews, analyzes, and appraises current policies and practices across several developed countries with similar education policies—specifically Australia, Canada, New Zealand, the United Kingdom, and the United States of America—countries that I visit often, in which I have many colleagues and contemporaries, and which have been the focus of my recent research activities. The policy examples cited throughout the book resonate among all of them.

Besides this, the book takes a broader view. It examines what is happening in the world within, around, and beyond education and questions what these activities might hold for the future—it exposes their "game-changing" tendencies and canvasses their possibilities. The unsustainability of existing educational leadership and business behaviors is explored through examination of emerging forms of education delivery, new types of educational institutions, and untested practices that portend further policy dilemmas and nascent leadership responses.

The book extends research on organizational change in education institutions and responses to critical transformations in education policy and practice created by globalization. There is insufficient consideration of policy paradox, especially that pertaining to educational leadership, business, and governance. *Education Game-Changers* attempts to fill some of this research gap.

The book chronicles the current chaotic policy environment and ponders possibilities and pitfalls that cannot be ignored by instrumental players such as governments, policy makers, educational leaders and governors, education business managers, and researchers and analysts. Many of the issues and activities raised cannot go beyond a cursory mention, given the broad scope of this book. It raises, therefore, topics that require further investigation to heighten debate, discussion, and knowledge in the field, especially in areas that are being redefined by new players, policies, practices, and technologies.

I trust the book provides food for thought and debate within the messy arena of education policy.

Karen Starr
Boston, Massachusetts
October 2013

Acknowledgments

This book is dedicated to the people leading and managing educational institutions who informed the research on which it is based; to my Deakin University and professional colleagues, and the members of professional associations who add enormously to my job satisfaction; to my mother, Barbara Starr and sorely missed late father, John Starr; to Julia O'Brien and Jackie Ingleby for their invaluable research assistance; and last but not least, to Ian McDonald, whose patience and unwavering support go beyond any words I can express in appreciation.

Chapter One

Change, Challenge, and Paradox

Powerful, ubiquitous forces in education policy are creating unparalleled change on a global scale such that education, as we know it, will be entirely transformed within a very short time. Universities and training colleges will more likely be "virtual" than physical; schools and early learning centers more autonomous and diverse in offerings, operations, and values; while private tutoring, for-profit organizations, and home schooling will continue to increase in "market share." The signs of dramatic change are already evident. The "game-changers" are on the horizon or being implemented rapidly. The education scene cannot stay the same.

The astonishing disruption and exponential progress unfolding through the "second machine age" (Brynjolfsson, 1993) is spurred by globalization, challenging the responsiveness of governments, organizations, and individuals, as the world becomes smarter, faster, and smaller (Bush, 2008). Rapid change is defying prevailing customs, antagonizing current thinking, unsettling long-held traditions and assumptions, and fundamentally altering the way we live, work, produce, consume, and behave.

These recent developments present conundrums for educators and policy makers as they deal with game-changing, rule-breaking transformations to determine timely, relevant, and appropriate responses. These reactions are of profound importance because the phenomena at their source are altering education indelibly, and with enormous implications.

Globalization and technological change have intensified international economic competition, motivating governments to increase national growth, productivity, efficiency, and innovation. Education is seen to play a major role in enhancing national competitiveness and productivity in a global marketplace by increasing knowledge yield and ensuring a well-educated, effective workforce and citizenry (see Productivity Commission, 2013).

Governments of all persuasions have instigated ongoing structural reforms to align national education agendas with the demands of intensified global competition. As a result, education policies throughout the developed world have increasingly subsumed economistic imperatives to achieve national objectives. Current education policy is, therefore, heavily influenced by the needs, values, and underlying philosophy of global market economics and neoliberal political agendas.

Being a contested and highly controversial realm of social life, education policy reforms are deeply political, raising questions about the fundamental purposes of education. The global financial crisis (GFC) of 2007–2008 reinvigorated and fortified a *laissez-faire* economic and neoliberal policy hegemony, which has changed the operations and behaviors of education programs and institutions over the past three decades. Hence, education's role in national economic fortunes has assumed primacy over its individual, civic, or social benefits (Smyth & Shacklock, 2004).

The way we envisage, experience, and conduct learning and teaching will no longer rest on assumptions that have guided governments and populations for centuries. The twenty-first century will alter previous conceptions irrevocably. This book explains why and how. It highlights the turbulent times ahead for educators and those concerned with teaching, educational leadership, business, and governance in coming to grips with worldwide incongruities and inconsistencies in education policy that are pulling energies and resources in opposing directions.

This book is about the "big picture"—the macro national and international events and circumstances that will impact on the meso level—education systems and policy makers—with concomitant effects at the micro level—in the individual educational institutions that interpret and enact policy while working to remain relevant, rigorous, and viable. It is about the balancing acts, the catch-22s and the contradictions within change that create paradox, dilemmas, ironies, and enormous complexity, producing challenges and opportunities as education policy both shapes and responds to change.

First it is important to define some pertinent words and terms as they are used in this book.

GAME-CHANGERS

Dictionary definitions suggest that a game-changer completely changes the way that something is done, thought about, or made (*Macmillan Dictionary*, 2013). A game-changer is an event that occurs out of the blue—so unexpected that it is not even part of the odds (*Urban Dictionary*, 2013). The *Oxford English Dictionary* definition refers to an event, idea, or procedure that effects a significant shift in the current way of doing or thinking about something (Oxford University Press, 2013).

The *Business Dictionary* (2013), obviously representing a business perspective, similarly speaks about a transformation of accepted rules, processes, strategy, and management but goes on to add that a game-changer typically leads a movement of related businesses in the same direction.

In all likelihood, the meaning assigned to the term "game-changer" in sports leads to its original usage, that is, a sudden action—usually the result of a successful plan—that changes the entire course of the game (*Urban Dictionary*, 2013).

Game-changers fundamentally transform future developments. Synonyms include conversion, revision, renovation, alteration, adaptation, flux—yet none of these accurately capture the absolute, irrevocable nature of a game-changer, with the irretrievability of the past, the idea of "never-to-be-the-same-again" that the term implies.

The term "game-changer" may be considered to be a "buzzword," "jargon," a "geek word" (*The Ridiculous Business Jargon Dictionary*, 2013; The Office Life, 2013). The *Merriam-Webster* (2013), apparently the market leader in the dictionary business, lists "game-changer" as one of its top twenty-five newly added words, achieving dictionary status in 2008 at the same time as "e-reader," "tipping point," and "geocaching"; although a cliché (Italie, 2008), the term describes *something that radically changes a situation.*

PARADOX

In this text, "paradox" is taken to mean a seemingly self-contradictory or absurd proposition that when investigated proves to be explicable, well founded, or true (*Macquarie Dictionary, Oxford Dictionary*).

POLICY

Education Game-Changers uses the perceptions and sentiments of those who lead and manage education institutions to critique education policy as it pertains to their institutions and their work. The concept of "policy," however, is problematic. "Policy," as the word is generally used, refers to "a course or principle of action, adopted or proposed by a government, party, business or individual" (*Oxford Dictionary*, 2013). "Policy" is variously concerned with a direction, a stance, a platform, or a position that informs a set of actions toward institutionalizing a definitive goal and is predicated on regulation and control.

"Policy" in this sense, refers to the intention to institutionalize certain values and actions, usually developed and implemented in authoritarian ways. It is hierarchical in that policy is often developed and monitored by external authorities. Policy is part of the schemata of government, government agencies, organizations, and institutions (see for example, University of Sydney, 2011; Institute for Policy Studies, Johns Hopkins University, 2013).

This conservative policy definition refers to technical instruments by which social activities are directed. Policy aligns corporate goals with designated responsibilities for policy "implementation" (enactment) and monitoring to ensure that policy "implementers" meet intentions and stipulations. Certainly, this is a common, hegemonic understanding of what policy is, and this meaning is usually implied in public commentaries such as political addresses.

This neat, straightforward, prevailing logic does not concur with the conception of policy adopted in this book, however. Here it is accepted that the concept of policy cannot be treated as a tangible phenomenon in its definition, formation, or implementation.

Policies are not simply material artifacts or statements of formal intentions. Many philosophies, agendas, discourses, and activities comprise policy, making it *ad hoc* and messy. In terms of education, policy activities are imbued with political positions, demands, expectations, and compromises. And policy makers manipulate language and use data to promote specific aims and intentions, although policy authorship is rarely acknowledged.

Formal education policy decisions made by governments carry great weight and affect numerous people. But it is unrealistic to view the people affected as impartial players in a value-neutral exercise, and education institutions cannot be relied upon to accommodate policy intentions with the unerring fidelity that policy makers intend.

Those charged with policy implementation make varying interpretations, have unpredictable levels of commitment or endorsement, undertake and experience numerous other activities, have untold demands on their time, and have differing methods of undertaking change, some of which will be more "successful" than others. Those who receive and are responsible for enacting policy mandates may subvert, fundamentally alter, resist, or ignore recommended or necessary changes. If policy is unpopular, it can be distorted or disguised to fit real or perceived needs.

Policies, therefore, are processes and outcomes (Ball, 1994); hence, the policy process embodies a gamut of political influences that come to bear on policy from its formation through to practice. "Policy" refers to processes and outcomes that are "always in a state of 'becoming,' of 'was' and 'never was' and 'not quite'" (Ball, 1994, p. 16). As Raab states:

> In reality, everything is (at best) incremental or (at worst) a mess... It would be more surprising to find an orderly reality, with policies achieving their aims efficiently and without political contestation. (Raab, 1994, p. 8)

As a "bottom line," "[p]olicy is the legitimation of values" (Prunty, 1985, p. 136; see also Prunty, 1987), which immediately begs the question—whose values and toward what ends?

Policy makers have sought to manage and control education, educators, and educational institutions in all sectors and at every level with the aim of directing education toward transmitting a particular kind of culture (Connell, 1998; Giroux, 2013a, 2013b). Over the past three decades market imperatives have underpinned the education policies of governments of various persuasions—fundamentally they are driven by the same values and aims.

Policy contexts—historical, geographical, political, economic, and cultural—are important aspects of any analysis of education policy. However, globalizing policy discourses have created similarities in education policy "reforms" around the developed world. And yet there remain remnants of the conventions established in pre-globalization modernism, as policy—determined by governments that have to consider electorates and that often attempt to appeal to assumed commonly held values or widely held desires.

Regularly policies come and go so quickly only to be replaced with new aims and intentions. Incoming governments focusing on short-term political agendas change the education policies of their predecessors, often appealing to populist concerns through negative political and media commentary. A consequence is that education policy changes constantly, which makes full implementation impossible and policy effects inestimable while ensuring that educational institutions are constantly responding to externally imposed change.

With rapid technological innovation and stakeholders at every level and angle, emerging educational responses are often untested and disruptive to conventional practices and assumptions. Educational leaders are beset with interrelated policy demands in a context where there is no consistent view of policy aims or the problem that policy is designed to solve, and where "solutions" are variable and based on uncertain or nonexistent data. With no obvious intervention points or straightforward solutions, amid uncertainty and ambiguity with unimaginable consequences, policy can introduce "wicked problems."

Policy responses are made using fluctuating, complex data; involve numerous individuals, organizations, and stakeholders holding overlapping roles, conflicting goals, and values and exerting varying levels of pressure; and require decisions based on "best guesses" amid organizational constraints, cultures, and differing logics and world views (Horn, 2001; see also Conklin, 2005).

However, with policy fluidity, the longevity of formal policies, business models, and governance cycles have never been shorter and the work of educational leaders, education business managers, and governing councilors has never been more uncertain, experimental, and equivocal. Constant major change is the new norm, making leadership, management and governance more challenging, demanding, and inherently riskier.

Education policies and practices are expected to meet divergent aims and needs that often stand in contradiction or stark opposition to each other. Education policy aims can be so contradictory as to be hypocritical, producing unintended consequences. This is the focus of this book.

THE RESEARCH

This book is a result of several research projects with educational leaders and business managers in Australia, the United States, the UK, Canada, and New Zealand (Starr 2007, 2009, 2011b, 2012a, 2012b, 2013b, 2014b). These research projects were exercises in grounded theory building (Glaser & Straus, 1967). In this approach, theory is not derived deductively but rather emerges inductively through the data as they are gathered. Emerging research themes and unexpected ideas are analyzed and continually tested, producing further evidence and/or new theoretical insights (Corbin & Strauss, 2008).

This iterative process of developing claims and interpretations is responsive to research contexts and the multiple layers of meaning produced by the people within them (Gray, 2009). Data are validated when common themes recur throughout the data such that no new insights emerge. At that stage the data are "saturated," with subsequent interviews validating information from previous respondents.

Grounded theory building supports examination of individual standpoints within complex contexts and considers the inextricability of the macro, meso, and micro. Real-life experience is taken as a starting point that connects individual agents corporeally and emotionally to the structural, the social, and the historical. In other words, large-scale social structures affect tangible realities and therefore cannot be separated from contextualized practice or from the historicity of the period (Ball, 1994).

Throughout these research projects, common conflicting policy themes continued to arise. There were many issues emerging about education being straitjacketed by policy makers and politicians demanding certainty and externally devised, "surefire" ways of ensuring institutional improvement, higher standards, and enhanced levels of learning attainment. These tugged against areas of joy and hope and tales of learning improvements.

At the same time, research respondents expressed concern that education, education policy, and educational institutions were not keeping up with "the real world." They were frustrated about having to comply with one mandated policy only to find it made implementation of another conflicting policy extremely difficult. Some educational aims were clearly at odds with each other. These major themes about policy conflict have been the launching pad for this book. They have been augmented with a comprehensive literature review and public commentaries about education policy and practice.

The book consolidates concerns and controversies through a series of common policy contradictions overlaid with concerns about rapid technological, social, and cultural change and the huge impact these are having on education. It is written primarily for those who lead, manage, and govern education—the people who comprise its subject, who provided the data on which it is based, and who work to improve education institutions and for learners, teachers, and education communities.

ORGANIZATION OF THE BOOK

Chapter 2 interrogates the radical changes in education policy over recent decades that have reconceptualized education from a social "good" to a primary means of forging national economic imperatives. The chapter explains how and why this has occurred and the outcomes of this transition. Instances of governance autonomy and the devolution of authority to individual education institutions demonstrate how problem-solving and cost-saving efforts are pushed "down the line."

Chapter 3 discusses equity pursuits in education. These include programs of "massification" (education for the masses), diversification and inclusion (aiming to ensure the participation of students from all social, cultural, and capability groups) and expectations that every student can achieve and succeed. Equity is paradoxically jeopardized when competing with high stakes "excellence" policy pursuits. Education exalts student excellence, and assessment schemes attest to high achievements, but when infused with policy practices that punish those who do not achieve desired standards, then "excellence" can undermine equity in education.

The contents of chapter 4 dovetail with this discussion. Alongside massification, diversification, and inclusion comes coercion for improved outcomes and added imperatives of cost efficiency, savings, and heightened worker productivity. In the current context, a squeeze on budgets and inputs, driven by the requirements for greater efficiency, exist alongside policies demanding improved educational "outputs"/"yield" and outcomes (higher student grades/test results; higher research outputs; superior student/parent survey results; higher league table rankings)—or "productivity."

Education policy in a neoliberal/free-market context valorizes institutional autonomy, free from the strictures of government and bureaucracies.

Chapter 5 discusses how governments promoting the devolution of authority, localized autonomy, and decision making are, paradoxically, more instrumental than ever in controlling educational outcomes, policy, funding, and achievement targets.

The lean education bureaucracies of "small government" retain control by "steering at a distance" (Kickert, 1995) through heightened compliance, regulation, audit, testing, and other accountability regimes. While the rhetoric presumes greater power for local leaders through "distributed leadership," a center-periphery situation arises that positions site managers as disempowered perfunctory middle managers.

The contents of chapter 6 integrate with those of preceding chapters with its focus on instruction, learning, curriculum, and assessment. Chapter 6 interrogates demands for teaching and learning to be individualized to meet diverse student needs (individuation) while both teaching and learning are standardized through mandated curricula, testing and examination, evaluation, and appraisal regimes. The chapter discusses hierarchies developing within curricula, as courses are dependent on enrollment targets, as hegemonic scientific rationality infuses government policy, and as economic imperatives override educational objectives.

The chapter demonstrates how standardized testing narrows the curriculum and constrains educational outcomes, creates course and subject hierarchies, encourages "teaching to the test," and fosters institutional and individual competition while operating against cooperation and teamwork (Chilcott, 2014a, 2014b).

The conflation of "old-world" (industrial) thinking with "new-world" (digital) needs, practices, and aspirations that have made aspects of education outmoded, outdated, and constrained, are the focus of chapter 7. This chapter discusses changes that challenge current practice and render many practices obsolete.

Currently education business leaders ensure "green," sustainable operations to save precious resources and money. Funds are extracted from every possible means to create revenue streams and further cost efficiencies. Concurrently, however, there are pressures from governments to continue to grow, with economic growth being a constant pursuit. Education policy is complicit on both fronts. Chapter 8 discusses how these two contradictory pressures play out and are unsustainable in educational institutions.

Chapter 9 advances the conversation about pressures for growth and sustainability, efficiency, and productivity, by examining the effects on "human resources." It is assumed that people are an organization's most precious asset—effective personnel being pivotal to the entire enterprise, institutional reputation, and outcomes. However, the ability to save time and labor through technology, the pressures for growth, profit, responsiveness, and flexibility result in the intensification of educational work, the 24/7 nature of executive jobs, the increasing "casualization" of the education workforce, and continual "function creep" to ensure that a growing number of tasks are undertaken.

Ironically, it is in this no-frills, cost-cutting, lean and mean context that educational institutions are implementing workload or work-life balance policies, while stress-related sick leave, compensation claims and employee dissatisfaction grows among education workers.

Chapter 10 draws together the inexplicably linked discussion threads of the preceding chapters. It demonstrates how current policy paradoxes and problems in the form of contradictions and counterintuitive consequences abound, with their effects striking at the heart of education as many currently conceive it. Conversely, the phenomena spawned by rapid transformations can provide endless possibilities and opportunities. Either way portends a very different, perhaps unrecognizable, landscape for educational provision in the future.

This concluding chapter focuses on imminent issues that require immediate responses if education is to produce optimal outcomes for a very fast growing world.

Finally, given the broad expanse of topics covered, the book contains a comprehensive reference section. Many of the citations are also available online, even if only the hard copy is referenced.

Chapter Two

Economic Constraint versus Social Imperative

The first object of a wise government should be the education of the people.
—Egerton Ryerson

Better spend an extra hundred or two on your son's education, than leave it him in your will.
—George Eliot, *The Mill on the Floss*

Every man should have a college education in order to show him how little the thing is really worth.
—Elbert Hubbard

This chapter describes the policy transition of education from a social and personal "good" to a national economic imperative. The chapter explains why economic imperatives are dominant and resultant education policy shifts. It considers treasury pressures to reduce education spending (inputs) while demanding increased outcomes (outputs). Also discussed are emerging new players in education markets and perplexing developments that appear to cannibalize or undermine traditional education business models.

First, however, given the focus on education as an economic imperative and its maintenance as a viable public cost, it is important to understand that education is a business—BIG BUSINESS—yet many people are loath to perceive of education in business terms (Starr, 2012b). No matter what form it takes, where it is conducted or at what level, education globally is a multi-trillion-dollar industry.

Education employs millions of people and entails countless assets to supply the world's increasingly insatiable appetite for learning consumption and production. Formal education requirements consume much of individuals' lives, and knowledge is constantly expanding, making education an ongoing, lifelong pursuit. The overwhelming scale of demand for education across the globe is staggering. There will never be a time when education ceases to be an intensifying and integral component of life and work (Starr, 2012b).

In addition, there are the countless millions of ancillary enterprises built on supplying and servicing educational institutions and students. The gargantuan and voracious education industry feeds innumerable businesses and spawns others. Education provides jobs and creates them through its need for services, products, and facilities. While governments establish education budgets, the overall economy in education is unquantified and unknown. If estimable, the total financial activity alone would be mind-blowing (Starr, 2012b).

Education costs continually expand in line with community, employers' and governmental expectations. In the 1880s, for example, school class sizes were up to eighty students per class, in the 1960s they were around forty pupils per class, but now class numbers in the twenties or even lower are the norm in developed countries. Facilities and resources have improved and expectations have stretched as to what educational institutions should provide (Vaizey, 1962).

In terms of its cost, education can be classed in both consumption and investments terms—as a private and public good. Both individuals and the state invest (time, money, and resources) in education for the varying benefits they perceive it will yield in terms of their differing interests. It serves the political and economic purposes of governments and public policy makers to construct education in terms of consumption—a private good—when costs are to be reined in, but as an investment—a public good—when funding can be increased (Vaizey, 1962). The investment/consumption debate has been a longstanding contentious tussle, as may be gleaned from the quotations leading this chapter.

However, governments of all persuasions compromise their original philosophical stances and values, understanding that both left and right, the social and the economic, need each other. And there will always be arguments concerning what counts as an "investment" and what can be considered a "consumable," and about the balance between the two. In policy terms, governments have positioned education at varying times more as an investment or more as a consumable, depending on their needs and priorities—which comes down to budgets, political expediency, and policy priorities.

The current education funding focus is on outputs rather than inputs and a "hand up" rather than a "hand out." Across the developed world, public investment in education corresponds with treasury pressures to ensure value-for-money (VFM) in spending with return on investment being highlighted.

Deregulation practices have enabled new players to enter the education marketplace, with escalating market share. The rise of nimble, flexible, low cost, low bureaucracy, for profit education providers offering online or high-demand movable product in low rent changeable premises with incentivized enrollments and casually employed staff are challenging traditional educational institutions, which are highly regulated and expensive to operate and have extensive premises and infrastructure, tenured, unionized staff, rigid operational hours, and standard program offerings (see Twigg, 2013).

In the United States alone, this growing sector represents 8 percent of all postsecondary enrollments as online education services burgeon (*The Economist*, 2010). Unregulated education markets, such as the private tutoring industry, charging fees up to $100 per hour, are flourishing (ABC, 2011). Some governments are contemplating aiding this movement by appointing noneducators as CEOs (new leadership terminology) in educational institutions (for example, Preiss, 2013b). If implemented, this move would indicate an appreciation that educational leadership roles now equate with that of chief executive officers in the business sector and are more managerial than educational in focus, although many educators, unions, and professional associations strongly oppose this development.

Sponsors clamor for naming rights and corporate social responsibility recognition, seeking reputational benefits and future custom. There are public-private partnerships, cross-level education provisioning, and multiservice hub developments, which are changing the way education is delivered and operationalized. A growing number of families are deciding to opt out of formal schooling and home school their children. However, many nontraditional players in the deregulated education marketplace are not subjected to the same regulatory demands as their traditional counterparts.

Public education supporters and lobby groups oppose the privatization of education and private institutions, claiming they fundamentally separate social groups from each other and undermine social inclusion and the desirability of students from all social backgrounds learning together (Gillespie, 2014; Kynaston, 2013).

On the other hand, there are suggestions that wealthy parents should pay for their children to attend public (government) schools (Buckingham, 2014a, 2014b; Smith, 2014; see Dinham, 2014). Conservative thinkers argue that in an era of "budgetary constraints, it makes economic sense [that] high income earners should fund their children's schooling. Independent schools benefit the nation by providing choice, which is vital in a free society" (*The Australian*, 2013). And proponents of all political persuasions are increasingly choosing private education.

Anticapitalist filmmaker Michael Moore famously claimed he chose a private school in New York rather than the local state school (which required pupils to pass through a metal detector each day) because "our daughter is not the one to be sacrificed to make things better" (Young, 2013).

WHO PAYS FOR EDUCATION?

Luckily for current generations in developed nations, education is a provision of the state for all children in the compulsory years of schooling. The public pays for this provision through the taxation quantum, augmented by business credits, private donors, foundations, and philanthropic organizations.

Nations compete with each other to achieve the highest education rankings (which attracts status and international student trade), states and national regions compete with each other (with higher results attracting rewards—increased funding and status), districts compete with each other to improve their share of the funding pie (see for example, Brill, 2010), and individual institutions compete for reputational status, funds, resources, enrollments, and staff. As funding reaches individual institutions, the issue of "need" comes most sharply into focus. It is possible to see how each level of the education funding debate fuses into the other.

Education is inextricably implicated in debates and decisions about public spending, either in terms of its cost, or in terms of its benefits (consumption or investment). Governments tread a tightrope and have generally taken a conservative and restrained stance in response. In every country mentioned in this research, governments are concerned about national debt levels and how to reduce them in the face of increasing social demands and at a time when social expenditure rivals or exceeds tax revenue collections.

Some contend that government debt levels are only of concern if monies have been invested in the wrong things. If public monies are invested in long-lasting intergenerational infrastructure, then the issue of younger generations inheriting a debt may be justifiable. From this perspective, spending that does not address deteriorating infrastructure and depleted public services, such as high-cost education, is often considered unjustifiable or able to be put off until more lucrative circumstances arise.

Emphases of spending on education indicate that governments perceive that it is wiser to spend on the younger sector of populations (the future income source), rather than on older segments (a more cost-intensive group). Investments in early childhood education and cost reductions in student loans are similar indications of the future income and cost savings potential they hold.

However, at the time of writing, the world is still recovering from the global financial and economic crises of 2008, responding to multibillion-dollar debt bailouts in the Euro zone, without much history to go on in finding economic answers. Radical, creative and brave solutions have had to be found that deal not only with the symptoms but also with the underlying structural problems. Governments' responses have been to increase taxes, raise the retirement age, squeeze social benefits, reduce or induce growth through stimulus spending, and in education, make investment easier for the private sector (see for example, Heath, 2013; Productivity Commission, 2013).

Fray (2014) points out, however, that it is difficult for the person in the street to make sense of economic commentary because "it really depends who you talk to." Education looms high in debates about national debt—along with other social services, such as health and infrastructure (see for example, Emerson, 2013).

In the current economic climate, private providers are viewed more favorably, as they provide education services and alleviate pressure on the public purse as "user-pays" principles apply (see for example, Knott, 2014).

Many commentators point out that while there is strong support among the public for increased spending in education, the decline or "hollowing out" of the middle classes as a result of the global financial crisis diminishes investment hopes (see for example, Madland & Bunker, 2011). Societies with a strong middle class make the largest investments in areas of public good such as education.

The adoption of a more conservative stance, the fostering of market values and more stringent accountabilities in education, has been a common response in many countries (see chapter 5). This has entailed a focus on:

- market differentiation;
- individualism;
- consumer choice;
- institutional and international competition for outcomes;
- user-pays principles;
- cost efficiency and value for money;
- the installation of standards and benchmarking; and
- numerous regulatory controls and compliance mandates.

"Taming" education to respond to national economic and political pressures has taken precedence over social (investment) imperatives. An outcome has been intensified debates about who should pay for education, and for governments, how much and for what expected outcomes? The cost effectiveness of education comes into question.

COST EFFECTIVENESS

With governments in advanced economies spending approximately one-third of their budgets on education, fundamental assumptions about how education is organized and delivered continue to be called into question. Of particular controversy is the issue of cost effectiveness, and it is interesting to analyze the changing yardsticks by which perceptions of VFM are measured. For example, the Organization for Economic Cooperation and Development (OECD, 2013) cites the United States as being one of the world's biggest spenders in education—outlaying over $600 billion per year—but points out that much of the public money supporting education flows to the wealthiest students who are more likely to avail themselves of ongoing educational opportunities.

There are many commentators who rue the fact that, despite increasing education funding, student achievement has actually declined (Caldwell, 2013a, 2013b; Gates, 2011a, 2011b). Coulson (2011), for example, analyzed American standardized test data in school mathematics, reading, and science from 1970 to 2010 showing that student achievement remained steady over the forty-year period while costs escalated:

> In the face of concerted and unflagging efforts by Congress and the states, public schooling has suffered a massive productivity collapse — it now costs three times as much to provide essentially the same education as we provided in 1970. . . . The fact that outcomes have remained flat or declined while spending skyrocketed is a disaster unparalleled in any other field. (Coulson, 2011, p. 5)

Coulson (2011) also criticizes the failure of other national aims for education, including closing the achievement gap between socioeconomic and racial groups, where statistics largely remain unaltered.

Powerful philanthropic players such as Bill Gates of the Bill and Melinda Gates Foundation are also roaming into education territory and taking a growing role in education policy and practice. They, too, question why U.S. education results fall below those of other countries, even when the costs of education rise continually.

And while there are criticisms of private entrepreneurial outsiders with market-based "solutions" and "questionable investments" venturing into education policy and establishing alternative providers to rival traditional practices and institutions (see Zeichner & Pena-Sandoval, 2015), politicians also lament poor returns on education investment (declining standardized testing rankings) (Starr, 2014a; Tienken, 2014).

Concurrently, media and review reports declare college completion rates are falling, preschool enrollments are dropping, teacher salaries are becoming uncompetitive, budgets are being cut, while "the country is losing ground to other nations from pre-school through college" (Simon, 2013, p. 1; see also OECD, 2013).

In the current fiscal climate, many government agencies view budget allocations as too expensive to maintain (Brill, 2010; CESA, 2010). The most obvious paradox in government cost-cutting exercises is that reduced inputs occur at the same time that governments are expecting improved outputs. While education is a huge public expense, it also generates income and ensures public savings. Meanwhile, many privately funded institutions and elite global universities have the means to spend more and often do.

Wellman (2008) suggests the focus should be on how educational funds are spent, rather than on who pays, and asks: Is the money used to support teaching and learning? Is it going to the institutions catering to the majority of students? From this perspective, Wellman cites the severest cuts in higher education instruction as occurring in institutions catering the most to first-in-family and low-income students (who often require additional learning support), making equity problems more pronounced.

To overcome these problems, sights are focused on educational leaders, institutional governors, and policy makers: "To focus intently on student learning, teaching, and degree attainment, institutional and policy leaders need to connect the dots between spending and results and make spending on teaching and learning their first priority" (Wellman, 2008).

Education institutions compete for enrollments or "market share," devise means of distinguishing themselves from competitors or their "point of difference," conceive ways of raising standards and outputs or "continuous quality improvement," and keep a close eye on revenues and expenditure, or the bottom line. Every institution is in the same game, spurred by external accountabilities, rewards, and threats, while responding as best they can to their own internal issues, needs, and individual context. Costs matter at every level.

Concurrently, however, there are mounting pressures for educators to produce greater social and economic returns, raise education standards (as defined by commercial private testing agencies), and to find ways to do more with less. This is achieved through policy coercion, increasing accountabilities on educational leaders, and changing the psychology behind funding, with rewards going to high-achieving institutions and penalties or closure notices being handed out to failing institutions.

In these circumstances, forced institutional closures and mergers are common, as is the removal of educational leaders (see for example, Carlson, 2014; Richards, 2014; Tickle, 2012). A further example is the Obama administration's plan to address college costs via a rating system that ties financial aid to institutional performance ratings (see NACUBO, 2013).

The cost debate now stretches beyond the conventional years of education as parents and governments invest in creating "advantage." For example, prekindergarten is an emerging area of education policy in the United States, where a national experiment is opening prekindergartens for young children (see Moore, 2014; *The Economist*, 2013b).

Preschool provides a one-year program of play and school-preparation activities before children embark on school proper, but prekindergarten precedes preschool. It is a means for parents to provide their toddlers with a learning edge before they commence preschool and schooling. And it is a means of saving children from poor- to middle-income or immigrant families' from falling behind in schooling by giving them a head start.

Some claim that pre-K is expensive babysitting and a harmful and cruel way of taking children away from their parents at ever-earlier ages. Is this policy welfare or investment? Texas has decided it's the latter and is investing in its very young for the future (*The Economist*, 2013b). It is recruiting top teachers for pre-K centers (they are higher paid but more easily dispensable if they fail to meet expectations), with full-day classes to suit the needs of working parents. Parents taking advantage of the scheme must agree to read to their children daily and provide home support for the learning program.

While the pre-K study has popular support, to become a permanent service it must be seen to pay dividends for children, parents, the state, the nation's education system, and taxpayers.

Other funding plans for improvement are based on cost-benefit analyses. For example:

- a multi-million dollar program is launched to address a shortage of secondary teachers (ABC, 2013a);
- class sizes are increased to pay for teachers' professional learning (Tovey, 2013);
- high levels of illiteracy and innumeracy are overcome by closing schools with higher resourcing costs per student—mostly small schools—to fund literacy specialists (ABC, 2013b).

And there is no end to the means by which funding will be reined in or revenue increased at the micro and meso levels. Texas and Florida, for example, are developing low-cost bachelor degrees, with the rationale that costs saved through online learning and new institutional efficiencies can be passed on to students. Initially to be established in high-demand fields, these degrees will cost no more than $10,000 and are seen to solve problems of rising tuition costs, high student loan debt, and spiraling debt default rates.

Currently low-cost degrees are emerging in low-enrollment, low-cost courses where universities want to attract students. Solving another problem—that of noncompletion—is incorporated within the low-cost degrees program. Students are encouraged to "finish what you start" through university-wide poster advertising and through fee waivers kicking in for the last semester of their course.

A $10,000 public university degree doesn't compare with private universities' costs of up to $120,000 (Lewin, 2013b). This is a game-changing "no-brainer." The other side of the argument, however, is that the low-fee business model is not feasible across a university in its entirety—it would simply cost governments too much.

Fast-track degrees are also on the rise in order to raise productivity. The proliferation of two-year college degrees is rising, while fewer students are transferring into four-year courses. Every semester eliminated in a course is money saved.

Trimesters are replacing the semester system at some universities, enabling a longer tuition year, reducing students' cost in time and money, and providing a marked "point of difference" in a competitive higher education market. Institutions are luring international full-fee-paying students (ABC, 2013c). Other institutions have increased teaching loads in "effectiveness and efficiency" initiatives to reduce costs. However, Wellman (2008) argues that in general the price for students is rising, while the investment in their education is not.

But not all educational institutions are having a tough time. Those serving wealthy constituents are able to raise considerable funds beyond state and student fee provisions—sometimes into the millions (see for example, Hiatt, 2013). This very fortunate position masks the fact that, while some may be awash with funds—from endowments for example—many more institutions are struggling, with the gap between the wealthy and the poor increasing. Poorer institutions provide for poorer communities lacking the wherewithal to donate and with fewer means to provide for the learning success of students.

To alleviate budgetary shortfalls institutions are "cutting the coat to suit the cloth": cutting courses, selling assets, and instituting staff redundancies, with these activities expected to increase (see for example Bauerlien, 2013). Creed (2013), for example, states that most Australian universities have cut their course offerings by half and are now focusing on courses that are profitable and therefore viable.

In addition, and related to budget reduction woes, are struggles to improve student retention. Annual attrition costs each institution many thousands or millions of dollars, while raised retention rates bring in income and reduce outlays in recruitment and marketing.

However, tactics to reduce enrollment outflow may also incur costs such as providing one-on-one support for students, offering deferral and leave of absence options, and developing new cohorts of staff and programs (such as cultural ambassadors, program coordinators, mentoring programs, student academic skills and study advisors, student drop-in stations, and student welfare personnel).

Lederman (2013), reporting on financial game-changers and long-term business confidence within higher education institutions, argues that: "Hardly a day goes by without some author or commentator predicting that the end is nigh for higher education, or significant portions of it."

Those with the closest eyes on their own institutions' bottom lines are not particularly upbeat either. An *Inside Higher Ed and Gallup* survey of college and university business officers completed by 457 chief financial officers across the United States found that 73 percent were not strongly confident about the viability and sustainability of institutional financial models over five years. Sixty percent agreed that a significant number of higher education institutions are facing existential financial crisis.

Wellman refers to this as a "Houston, we have a problem" moment. "People who know what they are talking about think we have a problem down the road if some things don't get fixed" (Wellman in Lederman, 2013). Fewer CFOs want to raise current debt levels and more believe that new spending will be derived from budget reallocations, rather than from new sources of revenue (Lederman, 2013).

While there is confidence within the profession about the future of elite universities, this wanes for community colleges and nonflagship public universities. Richard Staisloff, a former business officer, sums up:

> They get that the business model isn't working, but they don't quite see the bridge to the next model. And they seem to have some concern that may be there isn't a bridge. (Cited in Lederman, 2013)

Sebastian Thrun, CEO and cofounder of Udacity (see chapter 7), made the controversial statement that only ten universities will rule higher education in fifty years.

Similarly Ernst & Young warns that no Australian university will survive past 2025 unless current business models change—the status quo is not economically sustainable (Bokor, 2012). Structural changes have occurred in the retail, entertainment, and media industries, and higher education is next (Bokor, 2012).

Other commentators present a more optimistic picture. Kemp and Norton (2014), for example, suggest that greater deregulation enables further differentiation in higher education, with universities being unrestricted in competing on research income and course price. And a deregulated higher education sector offers opportunities for the private sector (Bokor, 2012, p. 27). The downside is that de-regulation can lead to losses in market share just as easily as it can lead to growth. Recommended remedies include building firmer relationships with governments and industry, commercializing research and targeting enrollments in a limited number of niche courses, and research (Bokor, 2012).

On the revenue side, in 2012 there were over three-quarters of a million international students studying in U.S. colleges, with a 6 percent growth from 2011 to 2012, adding over $22 billion to the U.S. economy. While raising revenues (international students pay full tuition fees), this also raises concerns about the skill development of domestic students (see for example, Marklein, 2012).

Cost effectiveness is a difficult route to negotiate.

AN ISSUE OF NATIONAL INTEREST

In federated countries, education is the constitutional responsibility of the individual states or provinces. States or provinces are usually divided into regions that exercise a certain amount of autonomy (see chapter 5). In many countries, however, federal or national governments have become substantial players in determining funding provision and education policy.

It is in the national interest that the population as a whole be as highly educated as possible to aid national productivity in a competitive global market, to foster good citizenship, and to reduce reliance on social welfare systems. Hence the Obama administration has established the goal of having the world's greatest share of college graduates by 2020 (Kanter, 2011). Similarly, the Bill and Melinda Gates Foundation wants America's education systems to acquire double the current number of college graduates and move to the top of international education ranking over the next twenty years without spending more money (Kamenetz, 2013).

The Australian federal government's policy target is to have 40 percent of all 25- to 34-year-olds holding a bachelor degree or higher by 2025, including a 20 percent participation rate of students from low socioeconomic backgrounds (DEEWR, 2010). The UK government has a 40 percent floor target defining the minimum standard students are expected to achieve in the General Certificate of Secondary Education examinations (see Adams, 2013; DoE, 2010).

New Zealand's Ministry of Education aims for a 98 percent participation rate in quality preschool education by 2016. By 2017, New Zealand aims to have 55 percent of 25- to 34-year-olds with a postsecondary school qualification at Certificate Level 4 or above (New Zealand Government, 2012).

National aims being foisted on education by governments via policy coercion is not a new phenomenon. Government funding for education responds to perceived needs or crises, ranging in geneses and form. Reviews of recurrent grants as a proportion of total expenditure occur at district, state, and national levels, which all have consequence for those managing institutional budgets.

Funding approaches based on best practice, "basket of services," "per capita plus needs," and other schemes are debated, and inevitably bitter arguments about their merit and fairness ensue. The National Defense Education Act of 1958 was an early attempt by the U.S. Congress to intervene in the nation's schools to improve the quality of instruction in response to Russia's launching the *Sputnik* satellite. (In particular, the intervention was intended to raise the nation's capability in mathematics and science in the competition for space travel [Coulson, 2011]).

However, national governments can have a hard time muscling in on territory that is not within their constitutional preserve. They achieve influence through the provision of funding through tied grants to the states, territories, provinces, or regions for specific purposes designed to achieve national policy aims. Even when monies for education arrive in individual states, provinces, territories, or districts, it is then distributed to individual institutions, with similar issues at this meso level surrounding the divvying up of the total funding pie.

At each stage of funding initiation or transfer, the underlying politics are contentious. Education funding is fraught as governments and agencies at differing levels battle for policy supremacy and do battle with those at the receiving end of funds. No matter which political party, how much money is provided, or how it is distributed, it is impossible for policy makers, politicians, bureaucrats, or educational leaders to please everyone. This provides great grist for journalists and creates sensational media headlines.

An irony is that new governments invariably overturn education policies inherited from predecessor governments, changing critical areas including curriculum, funding, benchmarks, and standards in teaching, learning, and leadership to mark a new direction. In the wake of short policy life cycles and quick policy turnaround, there are complaints that schools and teachers are suffering from "reform fatigue" (Zyngier, 2011).

Hence, like it or not, governments have foisted policy changes on educational institutions that have made them more businesslike and attuned to economic imperatives (Bottery, 1994), although the transfer of business practices to the education sector has not been without its critics (see for example, Bush, 2008; Hallinger & Snidvongs, 2008; Reid, 2005; Smyth, 1993; Smyth & Shacklock, 2004). The contentious aspect is that it is difficult to put a market value on nonmaterial goods like education. When promoted or sold through market mechanisms, its meaning and value is changed. Education becomes a commercialized commodity.

Critics deride the effects of free-market values and neoliberal precepts in education, with competition between institutions often overriding cooperation, with "consumer" choice often diminishing the local in favor of the exotic, with deregulation inviting new players of varying quality, with benchmarking and comparative hierarchies eliding contextual differences, and so on—in short, the creation of an education market or "quasi-market" (since education markets are constrained by government intervention) (see for example, Ball, 1993a; Marginson, 2010; Ravitch, 2010).

Meanwhile, some deregulated, autonomous education institutions falling into budgetary arrears or becoming bankrupt and stories of funding abuses and misuses create increasing media frenzies (Balfour, 2012; Mickelburough, 2012; Preiss, 2012b; Tomazin, 2012; Topsfield, 2012a, 2012b, 2012c, 2012d, 2012e, 2012f; see also VIT, 2007).

THE NEW RELATIONSHIP BETWEEN THE STATE AND EDUCATION

The game-changers brought about through economic and political priorities are delivering a very different education landscape. The relationship of the state to education authorities and institutions is rapidly changing with concomitant changes in activities and behaviors at the institutional level. As government funding drops, education institutions make up for revenue shortfalls by finding new funding sources or reducing expenditure.

Education competes with other social services for government funding. Over decades, state support per student in public education institutions often declines, even as population increases ensure enrollment increases.

It is interesting to note the concurrent arrival of restructured and reduced education bureaucracies and policies of "default autonomy" that supposedly free educational leaders from systemic control. Through policies promoting autonomy and privatization, educational institutions can receive funds directly, avoiding expensive intermediaries and layers of bureaucracy and accountability.

Caldwell (2013a), for example, criticizes the command and control approaches of large education bureaucracies and their classic "power-coercive" models of change. He argues that funds should be paid directly to institutions wherever possible, saving millions of dollars in costs associated with regional and central bureaucracies.

Meanwhile, a light-footed, for-profit sector unencumbered with "red tape", bureaucratic oversight, and compliance is gaining market share and presenting substantial competition. Free schools in the UK, charter schools in the United States, and private, Catholic, and independent-public schools in Australia receive direct funding in a new era of school education provision. Critics argue that devolved authority creates savings while governments wash their hands of systemic problems and place responsibility for policy "success" at the site level, with educational leaders on limited employment contracts shouldering the outcomes.

Meanwhile controversy over teacher remuneration is constant—such as the general low status of educators compared to other qualified professionals and the constant specter of performance-related pay and an equally constant rejection of such schemes from teachers and their unions (see for example, Sellers, 2013). (Davis-Caterall [cited in Ferrari, 2013] claims that in the late 1970s teachers were paid the same as political backbenchers, but pay scales have slipped back dramatically ever since.)

The state wants more teachers and teachers of higher quality, but at the same time, deregulation and efficiency policies are thwarting these aims while educational leaders contend with the impact on educational institutions.

THE STUDENT AS AN ECONOMIC UNIT

Students are the major source of funding for educational institutions—not simply because they attract per capita funding from governments, but because in some cases they are a source of private funding, endowments, and voluntary charitable donations. The U.S. Senate Finance Committee, for example, queried the necessity of annual tuition fee increases in higher education institutions reporting an average of 20 percent increases in endowments of $500 million or more. Over 400 institutions were investigated in 2008 to ascertain whether revenue-raising activities fulfilled their charitable, public status, nonprofit status. That's on the receiving end.

On the paying end, part-time students in the UK are shunning higher education due to rising costs (Jobbins, 2013). Demand has dropped significantly as students weigh up costs against benefits. Student debt in the United States stands at over $1 trillion and almost 54 percent of degree holders are either unemployed or underemployed. Two years after completing degrees, 40 percent of UK graduates are not in jobs requiring graduate qualifications (Walker, 2013; see also Maslen, 2013; U.S. Department of Education, 2014). Ironically, education debt is proving to be of little or no value, if no job exists at the end of it (as per the quotation by Elbert Hubbard at the head of this chapter).

The contract between learners and education providers and governments has changed. The student, along with the educational institution, is an economic unit who will incur costs for governments and themselves in order to receive an education. Increasingly, responsibility, risk, and expenses are borne by individuals. Walker (2013) concludes that the contract has broken down—there exists a crisis of confidence.

IN CONCLUSION

The reinvention of education has incurred concomitant changes to the social contract between individuals, institutions, and the state. The strong influence of the market, with its values supporting sovereign individualism, choice, competition, user-pays principles, efficiency, quality, and public accountability is fully installed. Innovation and entrepreneurialism are also evidenced, but clearly some institutions and some individuals will accomplish more than others.

The politically sensitive issue of education funding is "almost untouchable" (Young, 2013, p. 1). The current debate fuses issues concerning community, education as an essential social necessity and the common weal with those concerning economic imperatives and market values. If the latter course becomes the solid foundation on which education provision is built, then dramatic changes will incur more inequitable outcomes for the populace at large and more torment within educational institutions to remain economically sustainable.

This leads to a discussion on equity in education in the following chapter.

Chapter Three

Equity versus Excellence

Over several decades, educational researchers have demonstrated how education policies and practices are complicit in reproducing social disadvantage (see for example, Apple, 2004; Bowles & Gintis, 1976; Connell, Ashenden, Kessler & Dowsett, 1982; Giroux, 1981). They have also explained how education can be a vehicle for social equity improvements (see for example, Brown, Benkovitz, Muttillo & Urban, 2011; Darling-Hammond, 2006; MacBeath, Gray, Cullen, Frost, Steward & Swaffield, 2007).

It is paradoxical that education as an arena of competing interests and struggles can, paradoxically, be a medium through which agendas such as social inequality can be addressed, while also being an instrument through which social divisions and inequities are created and perpetuated.

Socioeconomic background, gender and disabilities, English language proficiency, and geographic location are some of the factors that have traditionally influenced educational access, inclusion, participation, and outcomes, reproducing social inequality and class divisions. There is also broad recognition that academic success is highly influenced by parents' level of education, socioeconomic circumstances and employment, the degree of family functionality, and by the social capital in both the household and community within which students live (Ball, 2010; Teese, Nicholas, Polesel & Helme, 2005; Topsfield, 2012g).

Social reproduction theorists highlight the role of education in maintaining capitalist relations of production and in reproducing the *status quo*, as well as the correspondence between education reform and the labor force needs of capitalism (Bowles & Gintis, 1976), now emphasized on a global platform.

Concerns about inequality have spurred many compensatory measures to be initiated in education. However, throughout the world huge differences exist between the top 10 percent and the bottom 10 percent of the population in educational outcomes, qualifications, and income (see for example, Clark, 2011). Much educational research demonstrates that social inequality diminishes the quality of life for all sectors of society. And despite governments' efforts to raise standards and levels of excellence, the more unequal a country, the poorer its national educational attainment record (Clark, 2011).

Social equity policies include a focus on "massification" (education for all—the masses), diversification and inclusion (with students from all social, cultural and ability groups expected to participate), differentiated resourcing based on need, and programs designed to enhance the learning achievement of all students irrespective of their background, interests, or ability levels (leading to recent policies concerning "individuation"—learning tailored to individual needs; see chapter 6).

Equal opportunities, social justice and equity policies, strategies promoting community and parental participation, partnership and outreach programs, targeted funding, and professional learning programs for educators to change pedagogical and institutional practices have been means by which governments and individual institutions have attempted to "make a difference" in social equity terms. In addition, there have been programs focused on "quality" teaching, for example, the Teach for America program aims to address teaching quality in poor urban schools (albeit, not without its critics) (see Schneider, 2011).

However, despite numerous policies, legislative interventions, and workplace practices, educational inequality continues to operate—equity in education remains an unachieved goal. Due to the power of hegemonic social values, some inequalities are so structurally and/or historically entrenched and naturalized as to be generally unperceivable or accepted as the norm (Hearn & Parkin, 2007). Hence, the organizational cultures within education institutions perform a similar function to those elsewhere in everyday life.

Achieving more equitable outcomes in education usually entails provision of remediation, extension, and community-based programs with concomitant human and physical resource implications. In economic hard times, however, equity policies and the programs they spawn have been adapted to suit the times, with groups targeted for "equity support" being stringently defined with reductions in programs and resources—the U.S. Head Start program was diminished during sequestration budget cuts in 2013 (DeSaxe, 2013); additional funding for Australia's "targeted populations" required disabled students to demonstrate "multiple severe disabilities" before additional support was available (Starr, 1991).

While equity measures have received general acceptance and are pursued through education institutions at all levels, they exist concurrently with policies impelling the raising of standards, quality, and the pursuit of excellence to aid and augment national economic competitiveness and raise living standards. "Quality" and "excellence," however, are never defined and often make strange bedfellows.

As they are currently depicted, a paradox occurs when equity policies coexist with policies demanding excellence (see also Bowen, Kurzweil & Tobin, 2005; Schneider, 2011). It is impossible that all students will attain "excellent" outcomes using the very narrow measures currently used to define and determine excellence (a topic explored in chapter 6).

Unfortunately, while attracting, catering for, and supporting a diverse student enrollment is commendable, the activities implemented to support diversity are often not available or are not calibrated in "excellence metrics." What counts, is the old-fashioned definition of excellence—student learning outcomes as determined by national and international standardized test results focused on literacy, numeracy, and science.

It is possible, however, that education systems and institutions can achieve excellence in terms of meeting policy aims such as improved access, participation, and support for diverse student groups. It is also conceivable that every individual will have some talent, interest, or skill to be able to excel in individual ways and through varying means.

This chapter examines how the policy objectives of achieving equity and excellence can run counter to each other. It canvasses why educational inequality remains a doggedly persistent and resilient problem.

First, dominant conceptions of equity in education are explored in an attempt to position current education policy discourses before examining how excellence is pursued and measured at macro, meso, and micro levels and the subsequent effects.

"EQUITY"

The word "equity" is often heard in reference to markets—to net value or a share traded on the stock market. In dictionaries, "equity" is also described in terms of fairness, impartiality, and evenhandedness. In education discourse "equity" is rarely defined but generally relates to policies concerning antidiscrimination, social justice, equal opportunities, and meritocracy. One discussion paper suggests that achieving equity in education "will be achieved by changing the balance of the student population to reflect more closely the composition of the society as a whole" (DEET, 1990, p. 2).

Equity in education focuses on access, participation, inclusion, success, retention and completion, and closing the achievement gap. However, aims to bring about social change for a fairer, more just society present "wicked problems" for education policy makers and have generally failed (James, 2007)—irrespective of equity policy discourses and practices and their differing political and ideological bases.

The stance taken on equity in education has an enormous effect on curriculum, learning, teaching, school structures, and leadership. The strategies implemented to achieve educational equity can abate or exacerbate oppression and disadvantage and therefore should be scrutinized more thoroughly. Furthermore, we cannot talk about equity in education alone—the term can only be defined and described in relation to broader social, political, economic, and historical contexts.

There are no universally accepted definitions of equity—there are simply positions from the left to the right of political thought that give a broad, general picture in determining where educational policy stands and where particular equity initiatives are posited and the philosophy underpinning them (see Wren, 1986).

Equity from a conservative perspective is aligned with right-wing political ideology and laissez-faire, free enterprise economics and defends and preserves existing social conditions, arrangements, institutions, values, and social structures. Conservative equity rhetoric speaks to libertarian doctrines: individual freedom, free will, independence and freedom to speak and act and respects and bolsters competition between individuals.

Conservative individualism endorses what comes to individuals by chance—by birthright—which influences access to wealth, power, education, and opportunities, as well as chance associated with personal endowments, talents, and abilities pursued through equal opportunity policies, and equality before the law. Heroes are made of individuals born "on the wrong side of the tracks" who make good, and stories of self-made individuals are revered as examples demonstrating that everyone has the opportunity to acquire the advantages and status that society has to offer if they are industrious. Status and power are rewards based on merit—the acceptance that some individuals will achieve greater rewards than others, which operates as a form of desert or natural law (see Starr, 1991).

The conservative view of equity accepts, therefore, that there will be social inequalities, but that everyone should be given a fair go, through the provision of equal opportunities. Inherent in this is the acceptance that human beings can never be equal because individuals are born with different endowments, but sovereign individuals should have equal chances to capitalize on their talents and abilities (Sadurski, 1985).

Capitalist democracies in affluent times often have "positive discrimination" and aid programs for those at risk to enhance the concept of equal opportunities, especially in education. Equal opportunity is about equal opportunity in competition, which drives the development of programs giving some disadvantaged individuals a head start or extra support especially at the beginning of the "race." This is where equal opportunities policies for targeted groups and equality of access fit in.

The major problems with the conservative view of equity center on the implicit inequality in the dogma of competitive individualism and meritocracy—that some will succeed at the expense of others. Upholding the maintenance of an unjust status quo propagates criticism when it also tries to embody an interpretation and implementation of equity. Within capitalist societies there is an elemental inequality between social classes, which despite legislative rhetoric of "equal worth," produces profound social inequalities (suggestive of George Orwell's [1965] *Animal Farm*: "all animals are equal but some are more equal than others").

Individuals who hold the most power have greater access to civil liberties and social resources. And when the economy grows rapidly, divisions and inequalities between rich and poor increase, both nationally and internationally (Chomsky, 1992; Sandel, 2012; Stiglitz, 2012). The conservative commitment to equal opportunities, positive discrimination, and aid in the form of relief are safeguards functioning to curb the worst excesses of capitalism.

The fundamental aims of political liberalism have aspects in common with conservatism— freedom from oppressive governments, economic freedom in the free-enterprise marketplace, and intellectual freedom of speech, belief, and religion. (In modern-day politics, liberalism translates into liberal democracy, which traditionally aims to limit the power and size of government, protect human rights and freedom, encourage individual responsibilities, and respond to diversity through market choice, while providing standard opportunities for everyone to achieve their potential.)

In the classic liberal stance, equity equates to fairness, which is seen to be possible to achieve within current social and political structures. A strategy can be "fair" if everyone, including the disadvantaged is better off (Lebacqz, 1986; Rawls, 1972). This does not mean that everyone has to be treated equally, which in education requires delivering different programs and resources as determined by students' individual learning needs (Schnieder, 2011).

Liberals emphasize the development of self-esteem, individual worth, and an ethos of tolerance, acceptance, and valuing of all people. The liberal ideal is full participation in society for every individual, leading to greater social equity and cohesion.

The importance of the individual in the liberal tradition is imbued with notions of individual rights, rationality, choice, and responsibility. Both individual autonomy—the knowing, self-present, sovereign protagonist—and the value of autonomous decision making and self-fulfillment are accorded high priority in advancing the freedom of the individual. This means that basic human rights and the promise of full sovereign autonomy are extended to all (Rawls, 1972). In education, liberal policies therefore promote inclusion, access and participation, and individualized learning programs.

Contemporary liberalism supports the development of "inclusive" practices and preferential treatment (affirmative action or positive discrimination) in the short-term to aid equity pursuits. Thanks primarily to liberal equity activists, *de jure* discrimination (discrimination evident in the law and legislation) has been and is being addressed, although *de facto* discrimination (actual, lived discrimination) is still alive and well.

The major problems associated with liberalism concern the stress on individualism. In free-market capitalism, different ways of thinking represent different class interests and values, determined ultimately by the conflict of interests and power relations within capital and labor. There is a connection between ideology, material interests, and the reproduction of specific forms of unequal power relations in society, with the relationship between capital and labor often not the free contract between rational, sovereign individuals as purported. The suggestion that individual lives are unfettered by their background ignores the notion of "social capital."

Further, liberal moves towards "inclusivity" and notions of engendering acceptance and tolerance among peoples do not address the incontrovertible discord between the advantaged and the disadvantaged. Liberalism is reformist, not revolutionary.

A socialist left political view of equity denounces both conservatism and liberalism as not only failing to address the fundamental causes of social injustice but as maintaining and exacerbating them. The socialist definition of equality goes beyond the conservative "equal opportunities," "equal access" and the liberal "inclusivity" stance and generally pursues strategies aiming at equal worth and equal power.

From this perspective, social equity involves collective emancipation and cooperation and opposes competitive individualism. It does not support the kind of equity that incurs freedom, power, and privilege for some at the expense of others. The redistribution of social wealth to remove oppressive social structures and conditions is seen as a moral obligation, and education is a prime vehicle for this to occur.

This perspective of equity is located within a conflict theory of society. Social injustice is the tipping of the odds constantly in the favor of particular contenders. Hence, approaches grounded in economic rationalism, which work within the established social order and reify existing authority and power relations, are condemned as foreclosing the possibility of transforming social life to alleviate inequality and oppression.

From a socialist perspective the *status quo* prevents the manifestation of values such as justice, equality, and the ability of groups to be self-determining—with the collective good being superior to, and transcending, individual and personal needs and acts. In education, this means that natural abilities should be developed to the fullest potential in every human being as common assets, with everyone having a part to play in society.

This social reconstructionist perspective supports education that interrogates the ways in which social actors have unwittingly participated in and perpetuated their own oppression (Habermas, 1987). This means giving students the skills to be fully active in society. It means a lot of heavy traffic between schools and their communities, participatory decision making, and student involvement in learning projects that can have tangible outcomes. It implies learning powers of critical inquiry and analysis, working collectively, critical reflection, problem posing and having power within the learning situation.

The socialist left questions whose interests are served by social structures and events, and at whose expense. It views social arrangements as temporal and capable of being redefined and renegotiated—the current social structure is only one of many social possibilities. Hence, it supports "emancipatory praxis"—the formation and undertaking of strategic collective political action informed by theory and vice versa. This involves reflective reconstruction with all groups having the freedom to control and shape their social situations, rather than accepting control imposed by others.

The view of equity from the left suggests that it is a historical quest—a quest that is contextual and continually in need of definition, critique, and contestation.

General criticisms of the socialist-left perspective concern apprehensions about the ability of human beings to achieve or even perceive a socially just society, while power and the desires of human nature will always limit and compromise this idealist position (Hayek, 1949, 1979b).

These three generalized positions on equity serve as a rough guide to analyze the political sanctions embedded within current education equity strategies and policies in education. These descriptions will also help highlight policy inconsistencies, in that strategies associated with one position may be substantiated by language and concepts appropriated from another.

POSITIONING EDUCATION "EQUITY" POLICIES

Using these three basic frames as the basis for analysis, it is possible to see elements from all perspectives within current education equity policies and strategies. Conservative perspectives prevail, although there is no policy consistency. While different interests have had more political sway over others at different times, conservative forms of equity have had more long-term appeal. Rarely however, are the underlying values and principles behind education equity policy explained and justified or the words defined.

The 1980s heralded radical neoliberalism and classical free-market economics as the mechanisms underpinning government policy and the production, consumption, and distribution of goods and services, including education. In a free-market economic and neoliberal political hegemony, equity agendas have become more sidelined.

The free market and neoliberalism have inwrought assumptions about equity, human behavior, and "society." For example, Nobel Prize winner Friedrich Hayek (1949, 1979a) uses the analogy of a game to describe free-market theory, which he assumes to be the game of life that he calls "catallaxy." The basis of this game is the belief that individuals should be free to pursue their own interests in competition with others, enabling the whole community to benefit through increased production, consumption, and innovation.

Inherent in the game of catallaxy is a psycho-social element, suggesting that interference in natural competition in the form of compensatory policies or handouts from governments skew and hinder the game by creating dependencies and serving as disincentives, thereby creating inferior social, economic, and individual results.

From the free-market perspective, interference or intervention by the state disrupts the naturally occurring "spontaneous order" or "free hand" of the market, because in a market economy, individual preferences, trends, and prices serve as indicators or signals of both the demand and availability of goods and services. Therefore, the market should be left unhampered to respond to these trends. From this classical economic perspective, state intervention in the form of social benevolence and welfare destroy "extemporization," as well as freedom and liberty (Hayek, 1960, 1979b).

Supporting this line, Mises (in Birchenough, 1914, p. 62) argues that

> Civil government is no fit agency for the training of families or of souls . . . . Throw the people on their own resources in education as you did in industry; and be assured, that, in a nation, so full of intelligence and spirit, Freedom and Competition will give the same stimulus to improvement in our schools, as they have done in manufactures, our husbandry, our shipping, and our commerce.

It is presumed that the natural rules of the game of catallaxy instilled within competitive individualism will enable all to benefit, even though some individuals will gain more than others. The "trickle-down effect" is brought into play through this reasoning (Smith, 1776, 1869).

The free market encourages private ownership of property and the means of production as issues of sovereign freedom and hence the link between neoclassical economics and neoliberal politics, often referred to as "economic rationalism." Marginson (1993, p. 56) defines economic rationalism as: "the form of political rationality in which (paradoxically) the market economy is substituted for democratic politics and public planning as the system of production and coordination and the origin of social ethics." Furthermore,

"One of the most striking features of economic rationalism is its universalising aspect, whereby market economics 'colonises' non-economic areas of public policy and in so doing crowds out other knowledges and practices" (Marginson, 1993, pp. 63–64).

In other words, free-market economics inherently subsumes the political, since the market infiltrates all areas of human activity.

Governments responding to a global market and neoliberal agendas have consequently adopted a very conservative stance in equity pursuits in education. Some special measures are applied to targeted groups of students, and antiracism, antisexism, and antiharassment and discrimination policies are broad spread. "Education for all" is the current mantra, and appeals to equal opportunity sentiments while satisfying economistic goals, including raising productivity and international economic competitiveness while keeping students occupied in education rather than relying on welfare benefits.

"Free" education, however, now comes at a cost, with user-pays principles applying to many courses, especially in the training and higher education sectors (see Gillespie, 2014).

From a free-market perspective, social justice and equity—implying that some members of society are not as well off or as advantaged as others—is a fraudulent use of the word "justice" (Butler, 1983). Nobody has behaved in an unjust way because in the market order, "the overall outcome is completely unpredictable" (Butler, 1983, p. 88). According to Hayek, social justice is

> an intellectually unrespectable idea. . . . I have come to feel strongly that the greatest service I can render to my fellow men would be that I could make the speakers and writers among them thoroughly ashamed ever again to employ the term "social justice." (Hayek, in Butler, 1983, p. 105)

An obvious criticism of this stance is the problem of an unlevel playing field with no account taken of contextual matters over which people have no control, for example, the endowments of birthright or a lack of education or employment opportunities which impoverishes all of society (Hutton, 1995; Marginson, 1993).

Catallaxy is a game without a game plan but with firm values that are being increasingly entrenched in education. Catallaxy and extemporization are game-changers. Social justice and equity concepts are defined in terms of results, using outcomes-related terms via impact and performance indicators and represented through various comparable metrics for "excellence," a concept explored below.

"EXCELLENCE"

Contemporary reforms in education characterize current times as the "excellence for all era" (Schneider, 2011). At the macro and meso systemic and government levels a "stick-" rather than a "carrot"-policy approach has prevailed in the pursuit of educational excellence. These policy pursuits have focused on educational leadership, teacher quality, accountability, extensive reforms and restructurings, and standardized measurement instruments to align education with market principles.

Competitive, demand-driven education systems depend on metrics of excellence as a form of quality assurance. Hence much store has been placed on the implementation of national and statewide standardized testing regimes as a means of ensuring and promoting institutional accountability for learning outcomes—often referred to in policy texts as "impact indicators"—with equal emphasis on national positioning in global education ranking systems (a subject canvassed further in chapter 6).

Researchers such as Marcoulides and Heck (1990) highlight problems with the simultaneous pursuit of equity and excellence as education policy goals, with the two usually undergirded by differing imperatives. At the heart of equity policies are issues associated with democracy and the common good, while economic issues generally underpin the push for continually higher standards or excellence achieved through competitive individualism.

Policy statements often warrant excellence ambitions promoting productivity using equity discourses as justification (see for example, the DEECD, 2012, p. 3). And on the surface, many would argue that there is nothing wrong with pursuing both excellence and equity in education. In fact, wouldn't everyone want both? There is a problem, however, when the means used to attain one, paradoxically, frustrate the achievement of the other, as is currently the case.

Unfortunately measurements of education excellence have become accountability and performance yardsticks, contingent on a fixed and limited definition of excellence, which stands at odds with a consensus among educators about excellence and equity for all. As prescribed in current policy and practice, the attainment of both is impossible.

Giroux (2013a, 2013b) argues that through current policy pursuits, public education systems have, ironically, actually become weaker and less capable of preparing students for active workforce and civic participation in a democratic society. He refers to a "growing political and cultural illiteracy" or an "education deficit," with students less able to understand political and economic purposes, their role in democratic society, and concomitant notions of the common good (Giroux, 2013b, p. 29).

Education is high on political agendas, particularly in electioneering. And politicians focus primarily on raising standards, with equity measures generally taking second place.

THE COST OF "EQUITY" AND "EXCELLENCE"

Policy aims arising from equity and excellence pursuits invariably buy into concerns about costs. Equity provisioning requires individualized programming, expanded learning pathways, and professional learning support for teachers, to name a few routes. Governments remonstrate about existing exorbitant costs and condemn educators for not being able to achieve higher results within existing means (see for example, Bonnor, 2013; Paton, 2013).

And the public wants extended provisions and a raising of standards, but much of this gets back to "who pays?" (see chapter 2). Rarely, however, is the cost of excellence policies in the form of standardized testing and institutional reviews and audits taken into account.

As discussed in chapter 2, governments walk a tightrope in education-funding exercises and, therefore, in equity policy decisions. Of course, the policies themselves, no matter how well meaning and, irrespective of the initiating government, can be critiqued in their own right, with each being inherently politically and ideologically biased. Focusing on the monetary cost of equity provisioning through resourcing actually misses the point. Ultimately, inequality is connected to broader social issues.

While education "markets," individualism, and consumer choice are encouraged, these emphases conflict with equity aims. Choice is exercised by those who have means (with institutional choice being dependent on factors such as location, religion, and affordability as well as perceived quality and reputation). For many, choice in education is out of the question (see Campbell, Proctor & Sherington, 2009; Firth & Huntley, 2014).

Educationally disadvantaged students are highly likely to be concentrated in specific localities and particular educational institutions. For example, Duan (2013) and Preston (2013) argue there are fewer "disadvantaged" students in independent (privately operated) schools and in Ivy League universities.

And in a market-driven system that thrives on competition through comparative results, enrollees matter. Students influence both institutional and reputational outcomes and hence market outcomes—there is evidence that the collective impact of educational advantage or disadvantage within an institution can have a concomitant positive or negative influence on individual student achievements (Teese, 2011; Nous Group, 2011). But a focus on the market impact of students is offensive to educators who focus instead on students' educational needs and outcomes irrespective of their background as an equity issue.

This situation, in and of itself, is an incontrovertible inequity. Choice and competition undermine communities, the common weal, social cohesion, and equity pursuits in education as Belfield & Leven (2002) assert:

> There is some evidence that—given more choices over schools—families prefer to opt for enrolment in schools that are of the same racial group as their own. Also, many families wish to enrol their children with peers of the highest possible capabilities and backgrounds.

Choice can also mean opting out of state sanctioned education institutions. Commentators argue that at the base of the growing home schooling movement is the view that government intervention in education promulgates socialist values and political agendas that operate against liberty and traditional family and religious values (Grande, 2014; O'Keefe, 1986).

Those opposing equity provisioning see issues of student participation and achievement gaps as something to be tackled at the micro level—within individual educational institutions and families—and not at the meso-systemic level or the macro-national, political level (see for example, Grande, 2014). These arguments resonate with the sentiments of Hayek (1979a, 1979b), who suggests that government interventions attempting to produce social justice ultimately have a deleterious effect by entrenching an entitlement psychology that further disadvantages those they are intended to assist.

However, educators take equity issues seriously. At the basis of this dominant view among educators are values about social fairness over the birth lottery and the huge social, economic, and health dividends derived from free, secular, universal education provision.

By its very design, competition creates inequalities. And cost effectiveness, user-pays principles, and efficiency will have a greater impact on those less able to pay, afford, and consume, while sovereign individualism promotes self-interest, not the common weal or public spiritedness.

Add to this the managerialism attending neoliberal education policy and economic rationalist provisioning with inherent center-periphery hierarchies of policy making and policy implementation, and the resultant corporatism, commercialization, and commodification of education, and it is possible to see that equity pursuits are in a losing battle.

"Excellence"—albeit undefined, underdefined, or defined very poorly as the case appears to be—sits so much more comfortably with market aims and values and is naturally accorded higher priority in education policy. "Equity" therefore assumes a market flavor and subsumes market values and discourses.

The OECD suggests that to be effective in the long run, improvements in education need to enable all students to have access to quality education early, to stay in the education system until at least the end of upper-secondary education, and to obtain the skills and knowledge they will need for effective social and labor market integration (OECD, 2010b). And if socially disadvantaged students continue schooling through to higher education, "high- and low-entry students perform similarly; and in many instances students with lower entry scores perform as well as, if not better than, students who entered on higher grades" (Craven, 2014).

Others suggest that, to have greater success, education equity policies need to be implemented alongside welfare and housing programs that positively influence home life, the capabilities of parents, and standards of living in general. Education equity depends to a great extent on broad workforce participation, job security and good working conditions, adequate community housing, food security, and health policies (Hopkins, Reynolds & Gray, 2005; Miller Marsh & Turner-Vorbeck, 2010). This would address harsh criticisms such as Mitchell's (2013, p. 18): "Justifiably, experienced teachers are frustrated by the indifference of parents whose children start school with no experience of books, and parents who leave disciplinary problems, general knowledge and even providing breakfast to the schools."

Irrespective of policy aims and broad support for equity reforms over several decades, there has not been any significant headway. Educational institutions are of "notoriously slippery substance" (Schneider, 2011, p. 139) due to numerous incompatible internal and external forces for change. "Excellence for all" has failed because it is "characterized by—and complicated by—grand ambitions that manifested in top-down and outside-in efforts at system building" (Schneider, 2011, p. 139).

The investment and commitment to achieving equity in education reduces failure, both of individuals and of schools, while securing future national and international social, cultural, heritage, and economic benefits. Yet equity issues appear to be bigger than any education system can ever address. And when there is a fiscal crisis of the state, we get the kind of equity that is cost effective—basic welfare—which doesn't come anywhere near the conservative equal opportunities definition.

Adding excellence to the equation comes with pressures of competition and rankings, on a playing field that is far from level.

IN CONCLUSION

Education cannot be excellent and equitable in a marketized system: "Education policies frame [educational institutions] as ideally 'excellent and equitable.' It is an alluring vision that very few . . . would argue against. The problem is, it is simply a myth in our current system" (Savage, 2014).

Markets don't produce equity: They produce hierarchies and exacerbate inequalities. Current policy practices for measuring and pursuing education excellence serve to exacerbate and further entrench inequalities. Equity is always controversial in theory and imperfect in practice. Some forms of equity are just not achievable because they are at odds with the political and economic forces that shape our society. In terms of overall education performance, excellence strategies are reducing the capacity of educational institutions to achieve excellence. And whatever the perspective, achieving educational equity does not require a more relentless focus on testing for excellence.

Chapter Four

Efficiency versus Productivity

Each education institution adapts its business model to the environment in which it exists. In the current context, a squeeze on budgets and inputs driven by the requirements for greater efficiency has resulted in changes in practice to do more with less, while becoming more flexible, adaptable, and productive in fluid political and economic contexts, so as to survive amid greater competition and accountability to increasingly critical stakeholders.

Before discussing the debates surrounding these policies and practices and the paradox they create, it is important to define how the words "efficiency" and "productivity" are used in the current education policy context.

"EFFICIENCY"

"Efficiency," as the word is used in current policy and management literature, has a different meaning from definitions found in dictionaries. Meanings of efficiency traditionally referring to usefulness, helpfulness, or timeliness have been tweaked in business parlance to refer to organizational cost savings. Efficiency equates to cost cutting, cost-effectiveness, and saving time. The ultimate efficiency is a balanced budget that creates a surplus and identifies areas of cost neutrality, whereby new programs are created without cost imposts.

"Value for money" (VFM) refers to the optimum goal—an equilibrium between cost, productivity, and outcomes. That is, low costs, high productivity, and quality outcomes (Carr, 2010). For example, a simple means of raising efficiency in education occurs through increased student-to-staff ratios, with even small changes saving high salary costs or enabling the provision of time to conduct group professional learning and planning (see *The Age*, 2010).

But efficiency in education is not just about maximizing productivity and services within the available (or shrinking) resources. Efficiency is also measured in terms of "customer/consumer/client" (student/parent) satisfaction and loyalty, restructured management practices, such as devolved autonomy to the individual institution, the downsizing of the workforce, and the outsourcing of services or through changing the mix of permanent staff and contracted labor.

Institutional efficiency in education also embraces notions of institutional autonomy and organizational capacity building. Organizational capacity building concerns increasing staff capability at the local level or instilling coproduction models such as public-private partnerships or outsourcing services to reduce or alleviate reliance and support from central agencies (primarily governments), while keeping educational institutions focused on their "core business" of teaching and learning.

Currently, these forms of efficiency are promoted by political parties of all persuasions, due to their economic and budgetary benefits, with costs and responsibility transferred increasingly to the local level and a concomitant shift in the social contract from the collective to the individual or "the user."

"PRODUCTIVITY"

Productivity in organizational management is defined as a measure of efficiency of production. It equates ratios of inputs (for example, funding and resources) to outputs (in the case of education that is educational outcomes—usually calibrated in terms of student achievement, numbers of enrollments, graduates or research quantum). Increases in productivity can occur through reducing inputs or increasing outputs, or both.

Productivity in educational organizations is created through internal efficient (cost-effective) service provision, but also through finding ways of enabling greater access, increased usage (such as enrollment increases) or improved usage impact (such as student outcomes or organizational research output) (see for example, Houghton & Gruen, 2012). Productivity is also improved through technological, materials, and energy source developments, improved information and communications services, upgraded work practices, mechanization, or automation, which save costs or time.

There is increasing focus on external productivity indicators such as students' perceptions and learning outcomes and the individual activities of staff as calibrated through national and international achievement measurement schemes. Hence, customer relationships management (CRM), quality assurance (QA), and human resources management systems (HRMS) have been incorporated in efficiency and productivity pursuits in educational institutions.

Productivity is tied to accountability (see chapter 5). Accountability is increasingly construed in individual as well as organizational terms to demonstrate the personal activities and responsibilities that have contributed to the organization's overall performance (output). This can entail technological change or innovation such as a service or product creation or a contribution to a measurable output such as increased enrollments or positive student achievement. In education there is heavy reliance on externally imposed, comparative models of productivity analysis, both national and international.

Productivity equates to raising the financial health of an educational institution. Hence productivity is the measurable aspect of efficiency, which is a focus of formal accountability mechanisms. (It is not the sole focus of accountability, however—accountability also includes compliance or conformance as well as elements such as the attainment of "key performance indicators" in "key result areas" and the outcomes of professional judgment and initiative, as will be discussed in chapter 5.)

Productivity, in traditional economic terms, is presumed to increase the per capita standard of living. National productivity growth concerns standards of living increases generated through improvements in real income and, therefore, purchasing power. Real income is assumed to stimulate the economy through the increased capacity of individuals to purchase goods and services, make personal investments in health, education, leisure, and housing, with concomitant social and environmental improvements (Freeman, 2008).

Hence, governments refer to productivity in terms of economic growth, international competitiveness, and national performance required to retain or raise national living standards (see for example, Green, Toner & Agarwal, 2012). Productivity improvement is a constant focus of governments, and education is viewed as a prime vehicle for its achievement.

In recent decades, deregulation and faith in market forces have underwritten policy to drive improvements in efficiency and productivity. In education this has involved massive restructuring, with government policies focusing on:

- devolution of authority and institutional autonomy;
- privatization, downsizing, and corporatization;
- an emphasis on return on investment;
- public choice and organizational competition; consumer rights, charters and satisfaction guarantees;
- the implementation of user-pays principles and reductions in government entitlements;
- the privatization of risk as an individual responsibility (see Starr, 2012b); and

- quality assurance and accountability regimes; benchmarking and comparable data.

Governments have encouraged educational institutions to take greater responsibility for stewardship and operations, and hence partnerships (including with private organizations), networks, and collaborations have been promoted to achieve long- and short-term goals more effectively and efficiently (for example, through bulk purchasing to achieve economies of scale). And a continual policy emphasis on market psychology has been shown (individualism, choice, competition) to spawn "enterprise level" innovation, improvement, commitment, and employee cooperation and engagement and reduce welfare dependency.

The contributions of labor, capital, and technological innovation to total production or productivity are prioritized and calibrated at national, industry/sector, and institutional levels. Governments have ensured the commitment of educators to productivity agendas through coercive compliance and accountability measures, despite institutional autonomy (see chapter 5).

As education is a prime means through which national productivity is pursued, educational leadership has come into sharp focus as the means by which change and improvement can be channeled. Attention, therefore, is being paid to raising the capability of human resources, workforce planning, and skills developments.

As an example, the Australian government recognizes the rapid, remarkable economic growth of its northern Asian neighbors and their subsequent noteworthy educational attainments in international standardized testing regimes. The white paper, *Australia in the Asian Century*, describes Australia's future prosperity in terms of: "lifting our productivity and participation by investing in our most important resource, our people. Improving the capabilities of all Australians will raise our productivity" (Australian Government, 2012, p. 162).

And further:

> Our greatest responsibility is to invest in our people through skills and education to drive Australia's productivity performance and ensure that all Australians can participate and contribute. Capabilities particularly important for the Asian century include job-specific skills, scientific and technical excellence, adaptability and resilience. (Australian Government, 2012, p.2)

In total productivity, reforms are part of "value engineering."

EFFECTS OF THE EFFICIENCY/PRODUCTIVITY PARADOX IN EDUCATION

Measuring educational productivity is a science in and of itself. And while it is a prolific and expanding science, accounting for productivity growth is not a perfect science (Green et al., 2012). Flaws are to be found in assumptions about perfect market competition, variation in capacity utilization, and the quality and quantity of inputs and outputs, for example.

Economists may base assumptions on neoclassical economic theory, but many educators feel uneasy about efficiency and productivity policies and their underlying values being promulgated in education. In education, competition is not as highly regarded as cooperation; individualism is outweighed by concerns about community and teamwork; and cost-effectiveness is seen to diminish essential programs rather than enhance them. Governments, however, rue decades of increasing inputs (capital and labor) without evidence of corollary increases in outputs and so justify tough policy measures to lift performance and cut costs.

"Efficiency" and "productivity" do not sit well together. There is a paradox entrapped within these two, supposedly inextricably connected and compatible words. The paradox is a simple one: The more efficient an organization becomes (in terms of cost-effectiveness), the more likely it is that this efficiency will ultimately affect productivity (output/results) negatively. In other words, increasing efficiency may produce productivity decreases. Furthermore, if educational institutions become more efficient and productive, then the values underpinning education are open to criticism. Examples of the paradox abound as educational institutions attempt to do more with less, as is exposed in other chapters of this book.

Efficiency in the form of cost cutting has driven a number of significant changes in education—both in its workforce and in the "product" experienced by (and increasingly sold to) students. The use of technology to replace education employees (known as "re-engineering") has become commonplace—often implicit in downsizing—while the outsourcing of services has also assisted in achieving efficiency goals. (Outsourcing and downsizing often go hand in hand with "mothballing," or the sale of public assets such as land or facilities to effect efficiency and VFM.)

The practice of "workforce re-profiling" (replacing tenured, high-paid personnel with cheaper, less experienced staff or casual/sessional employees) is widespread. Ironically, both practices—re-engineering and re-profiling—compromise productivity and cost-effectiveness because it is cheaper to use qualified administrative staff to undertake administrative work than it is to impose "administrivia" on higher paid and administratively unqualified teaching/academic staff. However, casual workers may be less likely to work more than the hours for which they are paid, which also influences productivity negatively.

The casualized workforce is overwhelmingly female, with paid-by-the-hour workers having no certainty of ongoing employment and no access to entitlements such as recreation or sick leave, and with reduced purchasing power to contribute to national economic productivity. In addition, casual employees have few rights to institutionally funded professional development and training, which further limits their career development and, perhaps, productivity (see for example, Starr, 2013a).

As mentioned above, these employment practices have expanded administrative functions (administrivia) for remaining employees; DIY (do-it-yourself) tasks contribute to "function creep" (seemingly minor incremental tasks added to a workload that effectively change the type and extent of work functions and the nature of education work). These practices take time and focus away from teaching, learning, and knowledge creation, thereby reducing productivity.

Expanding tasks are invisible and are not taken into account in staffing or workload formulae, yet they are being constantly redistributed such that, if educators and educational leaders wish to remain focused on their main interests and perform them equally well, then concomitantly, their workload will increase. This is an "efficiency" and may appear to be a productivity increase, yet measurable outputs are likely compromised.

The unpaid overtime worked by education employees is not calibrated in efficiency exercises but should be. It creates huge savings for employing bodies and governments, but due to the serious ethical and moral questions it raises, this situation is "undiscussable" (Argyris, 1998). And these widespread practices are occurring as governments are demanding improved educational outputs and outcomes: higher student grades/test results, higher research outputs, superior student/parent survey results, and higher league table rankings (productivity).

However, governments are contending with further paradoxes in the quest for efficiency and productivity, with similar trends evident globally. Some more obvious efficiency and productivity problems are ignored yet have a knock-on effect in the broader economy. Examples abound:

- Twenty-five percent of Australians aged between 17 and 24 are not in education, training, or the workforce and are not actively looking for work, and in lower-socioeconomic groups, this rises to 40 percent (Sweet, 2013).
- Many highly educated young people cannot get a job because they lack experience or because the job market is saturated (see for example, *The Guardian*, 2013; Vedder, Denhart & Robe, 2013).

- Increasingly for the young, work experience and unpaid internships are replacing paid work and paid probationary work trials (UNESCO, 2012).
- Older workers with experience and dependability experience difficulties entering (or re-entering) the workforce because they lack current credentials or confront ageism (see for example, USAction Education Fund, 2011).
- Higher education is becoming less attractive to young people who cannot afford the fees or face the debt levels incurred through university course enrollment (see for example, Paton, 2010; McLeod, 2014).
- Universities in a deregulated market lower course entry requirements in courses leading to oversupplied employment markets in order to reap federal funding without due concern for the outcomes of graduates they serve. This practice is also accused of "dumbing down" education and training (Hil, 2012; Petre, 2013; Sloan, 2014).

IN CONCLUSION

The increased drive for national competitiveness on a global scale is fueling a growing preoccupation for students, teachers, academics, educational leaders, and educational institutions to be more efficient and productive. Much of what is important and valuable in education is being lost or overlooked in these obsessive ambitions.

Chapter Five

Autonomy versus Control

This chapter discusses a number of significant shifts in the regulation and deregulation of education leadership, business, management, and governance and the game-changing effects these shifts are having in determining education policy, provision, and accountability. It considers the contradiction in broad-scale policy rhetoric about democracy, autonomy, and "flat hierarchies" amid the magnification of bureaucracy and bureaucratic power, "corporatocracy," accountability, and surveillance mechanisms in education.

Consequently, educational leaders battle to address internal organizational needs for change when they are weighed down by incessant external impositions—a situation that takes time and focus from the educational enterprise and affects productivity.

This chapter discusses the logic behind the regulation-deregulation and reregulation of educational institutions; the changing relationships between government, public servants, and educational institutions; the power and positioning of educational leaders; and the effects of accountabilities on teaching, learning, educational leadership, and education business. It explains how autonomy and accountability are inextricably linked, albeit at times in paradoxical ways.

"AUTONOMY"

"Autonomy" is another word that has assumed new meanings in education as it is used to explain and justify new policy aims. The *Concise Oxford Dictionary* defines "autonomy" in terms of self-governance and freedom of personal liberties, speech, and will. The *Macquarie Dictionary* brings in the notion of independence, self-regulation, and pertinent to the discussion here, self-sufficiency.

Autonomy in education policy is defined and justified in positive ways—freedom, independence and localized control over decisions and resources. It endorses self-sufficiency coinciding with market values of self-determination and individualism, including individual responsibility for risk—implying responsibility for outcomes and consequences, good and bad.

Policies of autonomy for education institutions are presumed to encourage self-determined strategic planning and distinctiveness—"market differentiation" and "point of difference" to excel, innovate, and differentiate from "competitors." Being market driven, the assumption is that giving educational institutions autonomy while providing "consumers" with transparent information to exercise choice will raise standards and drive improvement through demand, grassroots decision making, and initiative.

Many countries have pursued policies of educational autonomy since the late decades of the last century, with their schools and training institutions now among the most deregulated and autonomous in the world (see for example, Machin & Silva, 2013; Napoli, 2013). Greater deregulation and policies of "default autonomy" refer decision making, risk management, accountability, and liability to site leaders and governors.

Shifts toward autonomous management have come under various names and guises, mostly being referred to as "devolution of authority," "decentralization," and "default autonomy"—which generally refer to a transfer of varying degrees of decision-making power, resource management, and governance oversight to the individual institution and its local community (see Caldwell, 2011, 2013a, who delineates three waves of incremental reforms over the decades).

The expectation in a free market, demand-driven, neoliberal context is that small government with fewer central interventions or strings attached to the provision or delivery of public services, institutes greater individual and local community responsibility to ensure attention is paid to local needs, goals, and associated risk management (Starr, 2012a). Inherent in the autonomy movement is the understanding that educational leaders, business managers, and governors will bear a level of responsibility in collaboration and cooperation with community members, "consumers," or stakeholders and that collectively they have the knowledge, skills, will, and wherewithal to drive improvement.

There has been widespread discussion about education autonomy policies, with both strong proponents (for example, Caldwell & Spinks, 1986; 1988) and opponents (see for example, Reid, 2013; Savage, 2014; Smyth, 1993). Proponents of increasing autonomy believe it aids educational improvement by increasing student learning attainment and raising standards (for example, OECD, 2010a). Opponents argue this policy move overloads educational leaders with myriad business-related problems that interfere with educational-related activities.

Opponents are also cynical about "default autonomy" occurring simultaneously with downward pressures on budgets and upward pressures on standards after governments themselves have failed to raise standards or reduce budgets—in other words, it is a case of problems being pushed "down the line" (for example, Marginson, 2010; Savage, 2014).

Caldwell (2011, 2013b) argues that the highest performing schools (according to international test rankings) have the highest levels of autonomy. These autonomous institutions are able to make major decisions on matters such as budgeting, resourcing, and staffing.

And many educational leaders are reported to be supportive of autonomy moves, stating that they appreciate decision-making independence and would not wish to return to more centralized arrangements, even though workloads are increased (Bullock & Thomas, 1997; DET, 2004). For example, the Western Australian Education minister is quoted as saying "I've never had one Independent Public School say: 'I don't like it, I want to go back'" (Collier cited in Topsfield, 2013b, p. 4), which suggests that autonomy makes educational leaders happier, the education workforce more fluid and flexible, while parents and students have greater choice.

On the contrary, however, the following findings in the schooling sector reported by OECD (2007, pp. 252–53) are noteworthy:

> After accounting for demographic and socio-economic background factors, school level autonomy indices... do not show a statistically significant association with school performance. However . . . [s]tudents in educational systems giving more autonomy to schools to choose textbooks, to determine course content, and to decide which courses to offer, tend to perform better regardless of whether the schools which individual students attend have higher degrees of autonomy or not. . . .
>
> Similarly, students in educational systems that give more autonomy to schools to formulate the school budget and to decide on budget allocations within the school tend to perform better regardless of whether the schools that individual students attend have higher degrees of autonomy or not. . . .
>
> School autonomy variables do not appear to have an impact on the relationship between socio-economic background and performance . . . greater school autonomy is not associated with a more inequitable distribution of learning opportunities.

There are also downsides to autonomy, with now countless examples of educational institutions that have closed, gone broke or fallen into receivership or damaged their reputations by airing their dirty linen in public (see for example, Balfour, 2012; Mickelburough, 2012; Preiss, 2012a; Tomazin, 2012; Topsfield, 2012a, 2012b, 2012c, 2012d, 2012e, 2012f). Front-page newspaper and high profile electronic media attention can last for several weeks, highlighting:

- that education facilities are community assets and there is a palpable sense of loss experienced by communities when they are forced to close due to poor business management and governance;
- the sense of belonging and pride experienced by students, parents, teachers, and alumni and the sadness that accompanies breaches of faith;
- the liability borne by governing councilors and educational leaders for safe stewardship and business decisions made on behalf of education communities; and
- that negligent, incompetent, and criminal business activities are experienced across all levels and sectors of education.

Fewer government impediments to operations, however, come at the price of increasing interventions in the form of new accountabilities, regulatory compliance, and mandatory audit reporting. Governments promoting autonomous educational institutions, "steer at a distance" (Kickert, 1995), mandating policy agendas and quality assurance mechanisms, devolving all operational activities to individual sites, and averting risk through intensive regulatory, compliance, audit, and accountability schemes.

Therefore, while bureaucracies may be smaller, government interventions in education are increasing: Deregulation and default autonomy paradoxically run parallel with policies pursuing greater external control through audit, accountability, regulation, and compliance regimes.

The respondents in research projects underpinning this book were well aware of drawbacks, with most criticisms concerning too much regulation and too many compliance and surveillance accountabilities. These come on top of constant restructuring and policy reform, and feelings that these activities are expanding and taking up too much time, while educational leaders have insufficient voice in determining major macro education decisions.

There is a further irony in the quick policy take-up of the term "educational leadership" over "management" when educational leadership is thwarted by tight accountability regimes and curriculum stipulations that render leadership sheerly transmissional or "any vision you like so long as it fits with ours" (Glatter, 2006, p. 71; see also Starr, 2014b).

ACCOUNTABILITY

Defining "accountability" is difficult since definitions expand as the word applies to increasingly more activities in education. The word, as used here and in education in general, means "to render an account of, to explain and to answer for" (Wagner, 1989). As Wagner (1989) asserts, this definition implies that someone is obliged or subject to providing an account.

Increasing institutional autonomy over the past three decades has been controlled through central strictures—stipulated priorities, regulations and methods of reporting alongside hierarchical lines of reporting—referred to from the 1980s as "corporate managerialism" (Marginson, 1997).

Another way of looking at autonomy is to view it as increasing responsibility devolved to educational leaders for oversight of the institution's educational program and professional learning of staff; resources—including finances, human resources, property and infrastructure; risk management—including duty of care and occupational health and safety; and short- and long-term stewardship, for enrollments, marketing, and public relations—with decreasing support from governments and education bureaucracies.

Promises of reduced red tape, fewer bureaucratic interventions and more authority to make decisions about curriculum and staffing at the institutional level have been a ruse.

Current agreements between governments and educational institutions in the form of contracts and compacts further ensure policy "deliverables" in return for funding and other systemic support. Under such agreements, educational leaders agree to adhere to government-mandated curriculum, policies, legislative requirements, regulations and guidelines and endorse the governmental vision for education while implementing their own strategic plans.

"Default autonomy policies" refers to increased trust, professionalism, inter-institutional networking, and local governance in exchange for increased accountability, stipulated in terms of producing improved learning outcomes and adherence to regulations and policy aims (for example, DEECD, 2012).

But self-governance only goes as far as overarching accountability policies, in the form of compliance and performance appraisals, allow. Autonomous education institutions are closely monitored, regularly inspected, surveyed, audited, reviewed, and tested, with requirements to furnish governments and other systemic authorities with continual, comparable performance information. Agreements or compacts rest on evidence-based improvement goals and efficient, effective leadership and resource management targets.

One of the major ways in which the work of educational leaders and business managers has changed (alongside drastic changes in the working lives of teachers and administrative staff) concerns these new dimensions of accountability and further demands for transparency and change for improvement (Ball, 1987, 1994; Grimmett & D'Amico, 2008; Marginson, Kaur & Sawir, 2011).

Education institutions exist within an "audit culture" (Power, 1997) which serves a fundamental role in social life—it is a means of social organization and control. "Audit" is difficult to define, given that it relates to numerous activities designed to test compliance, although the field itself is vast and vague. "Audit" applies to both general and highly specialized, idealistic activities—political, economic and cultural (Power, 1997).

Accountability is about accounting to others and being answerable (Wagner, 1989). Giving an account requires numerous obligatory activities: supplying data, disclosing information, providing explanations, preparing reports, satisfying reviewers, justifying actions for appraisals, and participating in numerous standardized test schemes—all of which come under the umbrella term "accountability."

Power (1999) also refers to the "audit implosion" as well as an "audit explosion," referring to the fact that institutional leaders, business managers, and governors in autonomous institutions now assume responsibility for enacting internal controls to reduce risk and ensure compliance, representing a shift in the location of compliance to a form of regulatory "internalization." This is "control of control" (Power, 1999).

Accountability measures infiltrate financial and nonfinancial outcomes of organizations, the activities of individuals employed to achieve them, and in education, the outcomes of recipients of the "service"—that is, students and parents.

An educational institution is audited for the efficiency of its financial management and accounting practices, for enrollment accuracy, for occupational health and safety adherence, for legislative observance, for policy compliance, for the accuracy and adequacy of its internal record keeping, for the comprehensiveness, efficacy, and execution of its programs and policies, and for the provision and effectiveness of its staff training activities.

On top of that are surveys and evaluations that document "consumer" opinion—such as parent or student satisfaction questionnaires and surveys eliciting evaluations about the quality of the teaching and learning program experienced. There are public service charters that create consumer expectations and delineate standards of service delivery. Just about everything in education evokes and entails "auditability" (Power, 1997).

Measurements are amenable to, and evoke rankings or meta measures in the form of league tables (see also chapter 6). These technical instruments attempt to constrain and tame complex educational processes by reducing them to simple, defined, comparable measurements. Purportedly accurate performance data allow the public and the government to consider each institution as an individual case, while being able to compare institutional results by means of "consistent" measures—standardization dressed up as individualization (see chapter 6).

Power (1997) establishes the 1980s as a turning point when auditing was promoted in a variety of areas beyond financial checking and took on new forms. Governments of all persuasions instigate and have perpetuated and extended surveillance developments entrenched as central to operations and control. He asks: How do we begin to understand a society, which seems to invest so heavily in such an instrument of regulation?

Governments around the world find accountability and audit instruments both seductive and inevitable since they serve legitimation and verification purposes. Outcomes-based and standardized performance measures have become the norm—even checks on checking processes—defined by external agencies, not by the practitioners who enact policy.

The impetus behind the push for higher standards and continuous improvement is the political purposes they serve. They are a response to globalization and appeal to hegemonic public sentiments about education at all levels. Political parties determine and legitimate education policy by appealing to broad perceptions about the quality of education at national and local levels, and the policies and practices so derived may not rely on research evidence, despite the faddishness of "evidence-based" policy.

The "audit culture" in education is purportedly rooted in risk aversion and compliance assurance, but the extent of these intrusions becomes detrimental when they assume so much primacy, take so much time, and change the nature of the educational experience, for students and educators.

New accountabilities also change relationships with governments inexorably through their new array of institutionalized and authorized checking methods, agents, and agencies (Power, 1997). While educational institutions are said to be more autonomous, their leaders and teachers/academics are under increasing scrutiny, surveillance, and accountability. As Craven (2014) asserts, "The teaching profession is subject to a significant level of scrutiny that few other professions encounter."

Hence accountability measures alter the organization of trust. Data about institutions and individuals are collected and monitored, but the underlying need to formally "check" implies a policy climate of mistrust, doubt and uncertainty. In any audit or review regime, trust is juxtaposed intrinsically with distrust—professionalism and good faith in an environment endorsing autonomy (trust) with safeguards to control and monitor professionals (distrust). Demands for quality improvements defined by external agencies reveal official distrust in the capabilities and professionalism of educators and educational leaders.

At extremes, forms of surveillance produce a psychological climate more likely to produce compliance, fear and conformity, stifling creativity (Robinson, 2010), problem raising, or challenges to policy rationale.

Individuals and groups are mandated to provide accounts of their actions to another party who forms judgments and reports on the information provided. These agents use their reports and judgments for various purposes—to create league tables or to provide rewards, further surveillance, or punishments.

Trust is more easily damaged or dismantled than it is produced or fostered. In this context, trust in relationships is often remote and removed and produces ripple effects throughout all sectors and levels. Implicit is the suggestion that the knowledge of politicians, bureaucrats, and public commentators is more valid and reliable than the skills, knowledge, and experience of practitioners.

Formalized accountability mechanisms are detailed, one-sided, and rarely challenged. The "inspected" must have confidence in those making assessments and the measures by which they make decisions and determinations, because, as Baier (1994) argues, matters of trust violation or malevolence are not easily proven.

The reputations of inspectors, auditors, reviewers, testers—those who examine, judge, report, and make pronouncements and recommendations—should also be under scrutiny to the extent that competence, reliability, and reputations are at stake—but this is rarely the case. Conversely, assessors as authenticators must trust the information provided and rely on it being collected and supplied by fair means.

Truth, honesty, and ethicality are underpinning assumptions (Wolnizer, 1987). For example, do those making quality assessments in education really know how improvements may be made, and have they ever been involved in such activities?

A recent push is for more serious consequences for failure to meet performance targets. The bar is being raised, annual reviews are tougher, and automatic rising through teacher pay scales based on longevity in the job are being questioned (see for example, Preiss, 2013b). It is no longer "business as usual" and there are consequences for slippages and poor reports. Australian government officials, for example, claim it will become more common for educational leaders to fail performance reviews with zero-tolerance policies for "under performance" (Preiss, 2013b).

Fines, litigation, damaged reputations, sackings, demotions, media denouncement, and public humiliation are the professional consequences, with little chance of redress. But corporate, clinical, and "cold" cultures lacking in trust, collaboration, and consultation do not bring out the best in people (Noddings, 2003).

Research respondents contend that much relevant information (and often information that is more relevant and important) is elided. Concerns include data reliability; invalid comparisons between educational institutions with very different missions, geographical locations, and enrollment intakes; varying data interpretations; the inevitable creation of league tables based on proxy indicators which may or may not accurately reflect quality in context; and the tendency toward the "lowest common denominator" as the basis for all new standards.

There is no two-way accountability. Central education authorities and governments are not held to account by those they serve, and quality assurance mechanisms to ensure data accuracy are not available for public scrutiny. Those who are checked are rarely able to evaluate those doing the checking whose authority and power is taken-for-granted.

Any assessments and judgments about quality—which are part of the armory to improve quality and raise standards—involve asymmetrical relations of power and information. Authority and authorized knowledge provides privileges concerning what information is valorized, who is entitled to know and find out, who has authority to speak and devise conclusions, and who can make decisions, take actions, and make policy pronouncements, based on entitlement underpinned by power and authorized knowledge.

"Paradoxically, the audit society threatens to become an increasingly closed society, albeit one whose declared programmatic foundation is openness and accountability" (Power, 1997, p. 128).

Accountabilities focused on quality present educational institutions with constant challenges to their social legitimacy and veracity (Hearit, 1995). Policy priorities are determined externally, while institutional scrutiny comes from multiple environments with social actors interpreting transparent data with varying levels of competencies to do so (see Hoffman & Ford, 2010). Hence, accountability measures have encountered a polarized reception based on differing philosophical positions, convictions, tensions, and fears.

Some critics liken accountability policy strictures to surveillance and Jeremy Bentham's (1995) "panoptican" prison (see for example, Shore & Roberts, 1993; Webb, Briscoe & Mussmann, 2009).

Shore and Roberts (1993, p. 1) describe this form of surveillance power in the UK's higher education quality assurance and quality assessment exercises as akin to a theater in which "each actor is alone, individualized and constantly visible" which functions to "control, classify and contain" educators. Furthermore the authors suggest that such practices are constructed "in accordance with a political agenda for social control and ideological reordering" (Shore & Roberts, 1993, p. 1), with subsequent limitations on intellectual and agential freedoms.

Educators and educational institutions are regulated within marketized policies promoting competition and choice while promoting performance pressure in the profession through "transparency" and educational inequality in the education "marketplace" (Savage, 2014; Webb, Briscoe & Mussmann 2009).

It might be expected that institutionalized inspection processes are not as severe or intensive as the continuous surveillance system symbolized by the panopticon—yet Edward Snowden's 2013 revelations about the hugely extensive, covert surveillance of ordinary citizens as well as world leaders may provide pause for thought.

Sheehy, Ferguson & Clough (2008) demonstrate, therefore, how surveillance practices are made easier and exacerbated in virtual education environments, adding ethical, social, and safety elements to considerations of audit and accountability. Technology provides the means for more intensive and extensive monitoring and auditing than ever before—controlling authorities have constant purview over institutions and educational leaders from every angle, and technology makes this easier.

Fears about "getting it right" and concerns about negative information being exposed through accountability exercises are risks for educational institutions. Subsequently, there has been increased spending for dedicated personnel and departments to oversee risk, compliance, and audit; such is the immensity, complexity, and time-consuming nature of tasks falling within this ambit. Accountability exercises add administrative burden and equate to "function-creep." They incur costs (direct and indirect) that could be put to educational purposes.

A further irony is that increased accountability requirements are occurring at a time when many educational institutions have down-sized, re-engineered or outsourced services, meaning that there are fewer available personnel to undertake these expanding technical, noneducational tasks (see chapter 4).

There were suggestions from respondents in this research that there should be an "audit of the audits" detailing the number, types, purposes, and consequences of audit/compliance/regulation/accountability activities required of educational institutions. The effects of accountability regimes on the work of educators and educational institutions are not taken into account by policy makers—although policies may have many negative effects.

"Autonomy" as played out in educational practice is not the kind of "autonomy" implied in dictionary definitions or the meaning commonly ascribed to the word. Through tight accountabilities tied to autonomy policies, educational leadership is reduced to a form of perfunctory middle management (Starr, 2007). This is despite the widespread adoption of notions of "distributed" or "shared" leadership in educational institutions, but with a control-and-command form of leadership operational between institutional and systemic/government leaders and decision makers (Starr, 2014b).

Traditional accountability systems do not allow educational leaders to appraise or comment on the performance of those above them in the systemic hierarchy. In reality a center or core-periphery power model operates. It is hierarchical and one-way and assumes power differentials between leaders and followers with decision-making authority at the top (Starr, 2014b). The focus on "raising standards" and aims to achieve "world class" education status internationally, are rooted in very traditional hierarchies of knowledge and power (Fitzgerald, 2012).

Hegemonic conceptions and assumptions about leadership are embedded within education accountability procedures, particularly those associated with individual performance appraisal systems that focus on policy goal attainment. Educational leaders with formal titles, and those at the top of organizational hierarchies in particular, bear the brunt of contending with institutional outcomes, even though they are not solely responsible for them.

This has concomitant implications for future job security, professional prospects and longevity in the role. The reverse situation is also true, however, as formal leaders receive much of the praise and acknowledgment when significant improvements are evident, yet it is not educational leaders alone who create educational improvements (Starr, 2014b).

Bushnell (2003) argues that educational reforms incurring greater compliance by monitoring the practices of teachers and educational leaders place them in an untenable position since "autonomy" policies actually reduce professional freedom and opportunities. A telling example is the OECD (2004) finding indicating that in Australia 76 percent of education decisions were determined and imposed by external bureaucracies.

Bushnell (2003) explains how educators, so intimidated by constant measurement and appraisal of their performance, compliance and accountability, surrender to policy demands, becoming complicit in their own subordination and limiting their prospects for resistance. Ball (1987, 1994) names the same phenomenon "performativity."

Kohl (2009) argues that controlling educators is deprofessionalizing and forces many to act against their own conscience, creating "joyless" institutions. Educators may disagree with education policy direction and many of the policies they are mandated to implement, but accountability mechanisms ensure their compliance (Starr, 2011a).

While the invisible hand of the market might be promoted in education as in other preserves, it is not an unfettered market. It is constrained and regulated by bureaucracies, irrespective of promises of small government and the removal of red tape. Governments are the final arbiters: they formulate education goals to align education with economic productivity and competitiveness agendas and determine policies to regulate the education market.

Just as "quality" is never defined, controlling audit and accountability regimes and processes they spawn usually fail to provide a fully developed theory of education or adequate underpinning aims. Honing in on how accountabilities are determined and how quality and excellence (see chapter 3) are measured provides insights into how politicians, policy makers and educational bureaucrats define these tricky concepts. The focus on student participation and engagement and quality learning and research outcomes narrows efforts toward understanding and capability building, down to crude calibrations.

Sophisticated audit instruments appear very unsophisticated from an educational perspective—they miss the point of education, confounding and impairing equity pursuits, while installing a hegemony of classification to determine and label who excels, who fails, who wins, who loses.

Accountability pursuits and measures are enjoyed by the "winners" and have become the means by which "winning" educational institutions both define and justify their existence (Fitzgerald, 2012; Olssen & Peters, 2005).

IN CONCLUSION

Audit and accountability mechanisms exist as means of power and control over individuals and institutions and permeate every aspect of organizational life even if disguised in policy discourses promoting greater freedom and autonomy (Selwyn, 2000). While they may exist purportedly to reduce or eliminate risk, create social certainty, and produce "evidence" for policy purposes, they run counter to and undermine autonomy and many educational aims.

Power (1997) suggests that the forms of accountability, the manner in which they are conducted, the style and forms of reporting, and the uses of reports all have a bearing on whether accountability is constructive or ultimately destructive:

> The audit society . . . endangers itself because it invests too heavily in shallow rituals of verification at the expense of other forms of organizational intelligence. In providing a lens for regulatory thought and action audit threatens to become a form of learned ignorance. (Power, 1997, p. 123)

Wagner (1989) suggests alternative forms of accountability in education that encourage students to become accountable for themselves, both in their studies and in life in general. That is, education will instill the kinds of values, capabilities and skills that enable educational aims to be met, focusing on inquiry, analysis, communication, reporting, explaining, justifying, problem solving, and so on.

The thought that stringently technical measurements that constitute the normative culture of organizational life are spilling over into the social sphere is worrying. This leads to questions about what kind of society we wish to live in. What sort of society mandates a checking-upon-checking imperative and what sort of culture does incessant checking produce? And who checks the checkers? While reasonable checks and balances should be in place, a culture of excessive accountability generates a "senseless allocation of scarce resources to surveillance activities and the sheer human exhaustion of existing under such conditions, both for those who check and those who are checked" (Power, 1997, p. 2).

The ultimate aim is the self-directed, self-initiating, self-correcting, self-disciplining, and compliant employee, who responds viscerally and intellectually to the quest for social organization and control. However, "techno-fixes" to control (Power, 1997, p. 128) rarely realize this desired effect and produce counterproductive cultures of fear and resentment.

Chapter 6 explores how quality assurance measures are pursued in teaching, learning and curriculum spheres of education.

Chapter Six

Individual Differentiation versus Standardization

At college age, you can tell who is best at taking tests and going to school, but you can't tell who the best people are. That worries the hell out of me.
—Barnaby C. Keeney

There is only one subject-matter for education, and it is Life in all its manifestations.
—Alfred North Whitehead

The measurement systems structured into education accountabilities and compliance obligations have also infiltrated teaching, learning, assessment, and educator appraisal processes. In teaching and learning, however, they create a paradox as policy aims for individualized programming, while requiring standardized programs to be able to measure and compare outputs. This chapter discusses the resultant dilemma by focusing on the example of international standardized student testing regimes.

INDIVIDUALIZATION/INDIVIDUATION

Individualization, or "individuation" as it is increasingly referred to, is about tailoring education programs to meet the particular needs and interests of individuals to achieve improved learning outcomes. "Individuation" can be defined as particularization, and specialization to tailor educational content, delivery, and support to meet the learning needs, aptitudes, interests, and preferred learning styles of individuals. Individuation recognizes that each student is unique and distinct from anyone else. No one can deny that individuals have unique attributes and characteristics that should be nurtured for their own and broader benefits.

Differentiated learning is expected to occur within regular classes with the role of teachers/academics being to differentiate the learning program to ensure all learners acquire the expected knowledge and/or skills to achieve prescriptive "standards" (irrespective of pedagogical method or learning style) that can be verified through learning assessments.

Individualized education programming has gone beyond its original remit of catering to students with disabilities, to span entire student populations. Remediation and extension programs, gifted and talented programs, peer-partnerships, mentoring, coaching and individual tutoring schemes, outreach and applied learning placements, cross-age instruction, and "flipped classrooms"—all emanate from the desire to better meet individual student learning needs.

Individualized programming of curriculum content and learning activities, the pedagogy and method of instruction, and the means by which students' learning is assessed are all open to modification to fine-tune education to suit the individual. New pedagogies, encouraging teaching teams to work in different ways with individuals or a group of students, derive from the need to differentiate facets of educational content and processes to best cater to a wide range of individuals in a class or group.

A further factor is to make learning relevant to students' lives and the society in which they live. The rationale is that learning should make sense to students, who should see the relevance and purposes of their learning in the "real world."

Individuation is a departure from the standard, the general and the universal—the factory, production line, or conveyor belt models of education that treat all students the same, even when their learning needs, interests, and aptitudes are different. It recognizes that finding one's strengths and interests is a part of identity formation that occurs through both formal and informal education, as well as extended learning to attain higher levels of excellence and capability.

While sounding good in theory, individuation in education is not without its critics. Reuchlin (1972) argues that taken to extremes, individuation based on special interests would risk being "populist," compromised by incomprehensiveness and a failure to appreciate realities and could lead to impoverished educational outcomes. Others argue that, while individuation appeals to democracy and individual freedoms, it is difficult to assess its "worthwhileness" and achievements (Gombrich, 2012).

There are concerns about extra costs for individualized delivery (see for example, Parrish & Wolman, 2004), and issues surround the abilities of individual teachers to cater adequately to diverse learning needs (Konza, 2008). And while individuation is being promoted, it is a fact that low enrollment or high-cost subjects are often eliminated from course offerings due to costs, thereby reducing the capacity of an institution to meet individual needs and interests.

A focus on the individual that detracts from the importance of the collective could also be seen to feed logically into the notion of "individualism" as promoted through market economics and neoliberalism.

Critics argue that society is a collective, both in definition and in reality, and that collectivity demands conformity, especially in ethics, values, economic policy, and even in academic disciplines. Others argue that the only way educational outcomes, institutions, and systems can be measured is through "standards" (see Quenemoen, Lehr, Thurlow & Massanari, 2001; Wagenaar, 2008).

Individualized programming, however, in the sense that each student should have learning experiences tailored to their needs, does receive a smoother reception among educators than policies that evoke competitive individualism. While being demanding of teachers, it is consistent with goals for educational equity and the rights of every student to optimal learning experiences and outcomes (see chapter 3).

STANDARDIZATION IN EDUCATION

The dictionary definition of a "standard" denotes "ordinariness," an "average," "average quality," "the commonplace"—which is also summed up by lexicographers as "middling" and "normal." Dictionary definitions also cite "banality," "mediocrity," "triviality," "pedestrianism." The word can also refer to a measure—presumably of "the norm" and to "conformity." The *Concise Oxford Dictionary* (The Oxford Dictionary Press, 1976) presents a more accurate definition of what, presumably, is meant by "standards" in education: A standard is a "measure to which others conform or by which the accuracy or quality of others is judged."

A standard is also a "degree of excellence . . . required for a particular purpose." "Standardization" in education refers to a particular determination of properties that can be compared with a standard and to which learning programs should conform. Through standards, notions of "excellence" can be determined (see chapter 3).

First, as an example of standardized quality improvement measures, the issue of standardized testing will be discussed. These audits of students' learning from early years through to higher education are prolific, and highly influential "quality" assessments are conducted worldwide, so the example is a pertinent one. Given the immense number of standardized tests conducted throughout every country, the discussion will focus on the PISA (Programme for International Student Assessment) testing regime for secondary students, which has global reach and thereby covers all the countries included in this book.

The chapter then discusses how these instruments contribute to criticisms about declining standards, while frustrating efforts to achieve educational equity and inclusion.

STANDARDIZATION THROUGH TESTING

Standardized test rankings were introduced only two decades ago by commercial publishing enterprises as a means of measuring and comparing institutional, state/provincial, national, and international education results (Kehm & Stensaker, 2009). Educational rankings against a standard involves three general processes: the collection of data against indicators; the scoring of data for each indicator; and the weighting and aggregation of the scores.

The rankings then become league tables of institutions, regions, states, or countries, ranked according to common indicators in descending order (Kehm & Stemsaker, 2009). League tables are formalized "pecking orders" of educational institutions and systems. They are very influential in determining:

- students' and parents' judgments about where to study;
- teachers' decisions about employment;
- research and industrial investment;
- philanthropic gifting decisions; and
- global partnerships and joint ventures.

The PISA evaluates participating education systems worldwide by testing a randomly chosen sample of fifteen-year-old students in mathematics, science, and reading. Introduced by the OECD, the PISA aims to assess students' application of skills and understandings learned during the compulsory years of schooling, to provide comparative data in order to assist education policy making and enable benchmarking exercises.

In 2012 there were approximately 28,000,000 eligible 15-year-olds in the 73 countries and economies (which includes individual cities) participating in PISA, with more than 510,000 students taking the tests, which represents a very small sample of 1.8 percent across the globe. Assessment tasks include multiple-choice questions and problem-solving exercises.

It is no surprise to learn that comparative measurement tools such as PISA have arrived at a time when the emphasis on student learning outcomes is increasing. There are many interconnected reasons why.

Globalization has intensified international economic competition with governments wanting to increase national productivity and efficiency via a well-educated, innovative workforce and citizenry (see chapter 2). International test scores from other nations and major world cities assist potential international students to make choices about where to study.

As argued in earlier chapters, the neoliberal shift to small government has entailed previously centralized tasks being transferred to the local institutional level. As a result, there has been a significant change in the nature of educational leadership since the 1990s. The policy shift to self-managing education institutions and small government brought about increasing demands for accountability, while governments' expectations about the return on education investment also intensified (see chapter 5).

Any spending increases needed to translate into greater "quality" (never defined), higher standards and improved student learning outcomes. Hence, although schools may be self-managing, they are under increasing scrutiny and surveillance through numerous compliance, regulatory, accountability, and audit regimes (see chapter 5). The introduction of PISA serves as a means of measuring education "quality" and school success, but it is also a way of comparing schools and schooling systems, while spurring competition between them, with the assumption that this will promote improvement, entrepreneurialism, and innovation.

This development has occurred concurrently with a growing consensus that it is no longer acceptable for some students to fail in school, unlike in the past where it was acknowledged that some less successful students would drop out of schooling. Schools are now charged with finding each student's strengths, interests, and learning needs. Policies demand that students succeed and realize their highest learning potential. Furthermore, schools are held to account for statements on their websites and in their policy documents (with litigation increasing), adding emphases to transparency and new accountabilities to a broad range of stakeholders.

A further factor contributing to the increasing emphasis on student learning outcomes is the politicization of education, with education policy being a major electoral bargaining chip, alongside "bad" press leveled at educators and schools as a legitimating exercise, giving the impression that education is in a perpetual state of crisis (see for example, Preiss, 2013a).

Standardized test scores are seen as measures of how a country is performing against economic competitors. For example, commentators opined that Australia "was one of only five countries, and the only high performing nation, to record a decline" in recent PISA scores (Harrison, 2012, p. 1). The then Prime Minister, Julia Gillard, argued that the country was "in danger of losing 'the education race' to its regional neighbors to the north, four of which—Shanghai, South Korea, Hong Kong and Singapore—make up—with Finland—the top five systems in the PISA tests" (cited in Harrison, 2012, p. 2).

A final reason for participation in PISA could simply be because a large number of countries are engaged in PISA testing (including all advanced economies), and evading participation could be construed as national defensiveness or self-doubting. If such a proposition held a grain of truth, then PISA participation may represent membership of an international "club" that is increasing in credibility and currency.

THE BENEFITS AND DISADVANTAGES OF PISA TESTING

The PISA tests are said to provide evidence of improvement or deterioration in student learning over time, place, and school context (OECD, 2012). Test results are indicative of progress over time (for example, performance in one year compared to the next) or across schools of similar type (for example, performance of one school compared to a school with similar attributes or in the same geographical area) or in light of new policies, practices, or personnel. Such data is very useful and provides evidence for introspection and educational praxis, with theory and practice viewed as essential in informing each other in education development (Grundy, 1987).

Hence PISA test results can be diagnostic and helpful in teaching and learning processes. We also know there is always room for improvement in every human enterprise, with none being more important than education. Test participation provides information on which decisions for improvement can be made with the aim of achieving higher outcomes (see for example, OECD, 2010a).

A further benefit, some believe, is that we owe it to students to make them aware of their true learning abilities and not to mollycoddle them through concerns about their self-esteem, luring them into a false sense of security if they are failing (see for example, Ng & Earl, 2008; Loveless, 2006; see also Chua, 2011). In other words, students and parents shouldn't be shielded from factual assessments of a child's performance and how it compares with that of a counterpart of the same age.

Education departments regularly introduce new curricular or promote particular pedagogical practices, so it is conceivable that governments would want some independent measures by which to gauge the impact of such radical curriculum and pedagogical changes. PISA tests might be one such indicative measure.

Governments recognize comparative student achievement data as a means of being transparent and accountable. Test results are understood to embody the effectiveness or not of governmental policies in education, in line with expectations concerning "evidence-based" and "outcomes-based" data to both inform and appraise policy.

Despite these advantages, however, extant research literature suggests there are many reasons why PISA and other forms of standardized testing should be viewed with skepticism.

The most common criticism is that the information derived from testing instruments adds little to what teachers already know. Teachers know what students know and can do and what they cannot. Teachers know what students must do to improve. In this sense, instruments like PISA deprofessionalize and "de-skill" teachers, with test data being privileged above teacher knowledge (see for example, McNeil, 2000). Valorizing "point in time" test results above teachers' ongoing professional judgments is not only disrespectful but costly.

A second common criticism is that tests don't account for the contextual differences that create educational advantage or disadvantage. Schools usually perform at levels that are indicative of the level of social capital they have available to them in the local community. Over decades, educational research has demonstrated that students may be advantaged or disadvantaged at school depending on their home circumstances (see for example, Connell, Ashenden, Kessler & Dowsett, 1982). Many factors such as socioeconomic background, household functionality, disability, language proficiency, or geographical location influence schooling outcomes.

Polesel, Dulfer and Turnbull (2012) argue that standardized testing has a disparaging impact on some students, some schools, and some communities, which is unconscionable when it comes to educating the nation's children and young people, while the OECD (2010a, p. 13) admits that:

> home background influences educational success, and schooling often appears to reinforce its effects. Although poor performance in school does not automatically follow from a disadvantaged socio economic background, the socio economic background of students and schools does appear to have a powerful influence on performance.

Hence, students from low socioeconomic backgrounds tend to achieve lower test scores than their advantaged counterparts. In light of this acknowledgment, PISA tests occur alongside a questionnaire delivered to students and principals to extract local information. However, these data are seldom the focus of national media reports and are rarely acted on by education systems on the basis of test results. On the contrary, poor performing schools can be punished for their failure (Ball, 1994).

A telling example is when politicians close failing schools and sack their principals (see for example, Grattan, Tomazin & Harrison, 2008; see also Reid, 2009). Ultimately, current practices generate new inequalities and entrench longstanding inequalities; rankings create a "continually increasing vertical diversification" (Teichler, 2009), providing stark academic distinctions between the rich and poor.

A third concern is that PISA tests only target certain areas of the curriculum and only certain elements within those curriculum areas. They foster a "core and options" basis for curriculum, valorizing mathematics, science, and reading above other areas of knowledge and capability, which suits some students and their interests more than others.

This reversion to a "core and options" curriculum model has displaced equal weighting in all curriculum areas in the compulsory years of schooling, which may disenfranchise students whose talents reside in the arts, humanities, languages, sports, or physical education, for example. In this way the interests and learning strengths of all students are less likely to be catered to, which is hardly compatible with individuation.

Hierarchies are developing within curricula as mandated curriculum models and testing apparatuses are narrow in focus. Curriculum constraint defeats the very outcomes governments purportedly seek and encourage in a free-market economy: entrepreneurialism, creativity, teamwork, critical discernment and choice, differentiation, and problem solving. The drive to standardize, test, and compare runs counter to current economic and workforce needs such that "new-world" organizations such as Apple and Google cite difficulty in finding employees who are creative, astute problem solvers, critical thinkers, and team players.

The media "beat-up" on education, educators, and educational practices has led to a regular public endorsement of calls for a back-to-basics no-frills policy stance at the same time that enormous pressures are being brought to bear to expand curriculum to solve a range of social woes—from road safety to consumer literacy. Hurst (2013, p. 1) refers to this as "a vision of the future—grounded in the past." Hence, a core and options curriculum model has resumed its traditionally entrenched position; a "center-periphery" model characterizes leadership and management practices (Starr, 1999).

There have been criticisms about teachers "teaching to the test" and thereby narrowing the curriculum (Chilcott, 2014b; Phelps, 2011; Polesel et al., 2012) and of schools encouraging slow learners to be absent for high-stakes tests in order to avoid lower aggregated school scores (for example, ACARA, 2012; Topsfield, 2012f). And there are teachers' guides (for example, Thomson, Hillman & De Bortoli, 2013a, 2013b) and students' test preparation texts available to yield a head start. For all the reasons above, PISA testing hardly occurs on a level playing field.

Evidence already suggests negative effects of accountability and quality instruments, such as standardized tests, resulting in narrowing the curriculum, "production line" teaching, and teaching to the test (Starr, 2014a); the labeling of institutions and neighborhoods through league tables; and the shaming, blaming, and great stress for students that goes along with league "naming." The tests evade essential learning dispositions such as problem-solving, teamwork, inquiry, and some things are difficult to test such as creativity, innovation, or higher order thinking.

Data-driven assessments obscure the benefits of formative assessments that teachers conduct as a regular part of their role and that are more informative than measures concentrating on literacy and numeracy. These day-to-day means by which teachers create a picture of their students' abilities and learning needs cover a broad range of activities: informal questioning, listening to students' explanations and summations, students' peer and self-assessments, learning aims clarification, material evidence and prompts, and providing informal feedback as learning progresses (Henderson, 2014).

Educators are skeptical about weighted aggregates of indicators being reduced to a single, all-embracing, boiled-down numerical score that purportedly encapsulates a quality assessment and a ranking against other institutions. Of further concern is the variance in indicators and weightings used to determine "quality" (Kehm & Stensaker, 2009).

At the macro level, PISA sample sizes for any country are too low to make judgments about entire education systems (for example, to fulfill OECD requirements, each country must draw a sample of a minimum of five thousand students only). And it is unlikely students across the world are studying the same material at the same ages/grade levels. Furthermore, test results do not indicate how improvements can be made. There are also concerns from teachers and their unions when test data are used as instruments to appraise teacher performance.

PISA testing regimes are costly in terms of their development, administration, analysis, and reporting. The funds used to participate in tests could likely achieve better learning outcomes if spent on teachers or learning resources closer to students and more attuned to their learning needs. But there are implicit institutional costs, also. Despite the rationale, ranking systems have profound effects on institutional behavior—promoting marketing, branding, use of consultants and professional agencies, and concomitantly, higher tuition fees. Students' and parents' expectations have also been raised, with "quality" and value for money being key (Dill, 2009).

From equity, professional, and sheer commonsense perspectives, standardized testing is divisive rather than ameliorative, encouraging competition, rather than collaboration and delivering many more negatives than benefits. Testing regimes such as PISA are esteemed as a form of legitimate global research, yet the valid findings of equity-focused educational research are marginalized in its wake.

For example, Amos (2013, p. A3) reporting on Ohio's standardized test results makes the salient observation that: "districts with straight A's (*sic*) in three most important measures on the report cards also had the highest average incomes in the region. . . . By contrast, districts with . . . higher poverty get F's (*sic*) on at least one of the three most important measures."

Quite rightly, low income schools claim that testing outcomes fail to reflect the complex challenges they face, while state report cards also fail to ensure public education is an "equalizer," providing children everywhere with opportunities despite their backgrounds and family circumstances (Amos, 2013, p. A3).

The power, hegemony, and control of quantitative methods diminishes critical achievements in student learning, teaching, and schooling (see chapter 5). Hogan and Donovan (2005) argue that decontextualized test results are indefensible in that they "[underestimate] the net contribution that schools make to individual wellbeing and aggregate social utility and [permit] a highly stratified and limited measure of school performance [and] academic achievement" (2005, p. 100).

Policy makers and treasury officials in Ohio, for example, argue that half the state's annual budget is spent on kindergarten-to-college education and, hence, want to see a return on that investment. So while some see standardized test statistics serving as a clarion call for more resources to be allocated to struggling schools, results can also be interpreted as educators failing to achieve expected results.

While schools should take notice of PISA and other standardized test results, they are not the be all and end all. Schools, in this example, should concentrate on their actual needs, collecting data from within to demonstrate improvements that have occurred, some of which may not relate to the formal curriculum (such as increased retention, attendance, sense of belonging, intercultural harmony, and integration of students with disabilities).

Data on all forms of improvement are useful for accountability, annual reporting, and school leaders' performance appraisals. Leaders need to account for all improvements and use them as an internal gauge of performance and for their own public relations exercises, rather than relying on external, narrow measurements and priorities.

Teaching and learning practices and outcomes have been standardized, rationalized, intensified, and made more "efficient," subjected to mistrust and disrespect, regulated and made to compete, brought to account, and scrutinized to achieve higher "quality" and raised standards in the interests of national political and economic goals.

Few other areas of social life would have experienced such pervasive intervention from politicians, bureaucrats, and consultants. (Some argue that occupations dominated by women—such as education—are subjected to greater control and political domination than others [Apple, 1992; Fitzgerald, White & Gunter, 2012; Franzway, Court & Connell, 1989]. This may be one explanation.)

Educational leaders should question why tests such as PISA are necessary and have the influence they do and should question the purposes to which the data are put and ask "who wants to know and why"?

While the setting of standards aims to present a yardstick by which learning can be measured, the use of standards and the processes of standardization frustrate efforts to tailor education to meet individual student needs and work against equity agendas. This is paradoxical, given that standards have been instigated to raise quality.

To meet expectations of raised standards, a new focus has been placed on teacher quality and educational leadership at all levels of education. Professional learning requirements, stricter performance appraisals, and measures by which educational leaders can more readily dismiss underperforming teachers or have them dismissed for below standard outcomes are parallel policy practices (see for example, Ferrari, 2013).

Policies change constantly, making long-term change difficult or impossible, with quality evaluations being rarely able to pin down cause-and-effect relationships between policy, policy processes, and "quality" undertakings by influential social actors at all levels. Likewise curriculum changes regularly.

For these reasons alone, it is impossible to make sweeping generalizations about the state of an education system based on test results alone. Test data focusing on one-year levels and making comparisons between cohorts of students from different countries and contexts present a very incomplete snapshot of education anywhere.

Standardized results are also equivocal. The Center for American Progress, for example, notes that national test results in mathematics and reading had declined over recent years, with over half of Boston's 127 schools raking among Massachusetts's lowest 20 percent. Showing how notions of educational "crises" are contextual, however, Wong and Shen (2013, p. A8) state that Boston schools are considered "among the best large urban systems in the nation," which indicates that education never seems to do well enough.

So, where should our focus be in terms of student learning outcomes? No one would dispute the need for a fundamental educational grounding in the three Rs. Literacy and numeracy are basic learnings that everyone would expect of any education system. When parents are asked what they want from schools, the three Rs are the most commonly cited need. But parents also want their children to be happy at school, to feel connected and not excluded or alienated by schooling processes (Starr, 2014a; Zeehandelaar & Northern, 2013).

While some parents may seek high test score results, most prefer their children to experience the joy of learning and to become lifelong learners. They also want skills that enhance employability, citizenship, and acceptance of cultural diversity and creativity (see for example, Zeehandelaar & Northern, 2013).

Employers seek thinking skills—both analytical and critical. They want future employees to be able to apply interdisciplinary knowledge to real-world problems, to demonstrate capacity for teamwork, take personal initiative and possess competent IT skills, intercultural understandings, and a can-do attitude (see for example, Career NZ, 2013)—and it is assumed that these are developed in schools.

Furthermore, successful student learning engagement achieves the highest rates of retention and attendance. In sum, the community wants students to receive a well-rounded education that values all fields of knowledge, that recognizes and builds on students' strengths and interests, in addition to providing a range of crosscurricular social learnings. This is the antithesis of the focus of standardized tests such as PISA, yet the prominence they receive from governments elides so much of what schools do and what communities expect from education.

The OECD (2010a) suggests there are factors that high performing and rapidly improving education systems have in common:

- High performing nations are clear about their commitment to education with citizens valuing education highly.
- Students study longer and harder in order to achieve at school.
- High achieving education systems set high standards and expectations that are accepted across the education system, with a focus on higher order thinking skills.
- Students are encouraged to succeed and do not progress through grade levels until they have mastered the requisite learning in each grade.
- The quality of teachers and principals is emphasized. Teachers are respected and importance is placed on teacher recruitment, training, induction, mentoring, professional learning and compensation.

Teachers work together to determine good practice and use research as evidence of the effectiveness of the approaches adopted. The most successful countries invest more money in education, prioritize quality within teaching, and use their most talented teachers for the most challenging classrooms (see also Harrison, 2012).

Experience in challenging circumstances is a criterion for career progression, as is peer-reviewed research. Furthermore, in the most highly successful nations and cities, the most resources are provided to socioeconomically disadvantaged schools. Systemically, there are high expectations for the success of every student and for the delivery of effective learning opportunities. None of these attributes of "high-performing" education systems has anything to do with standardization or emphases on testing regimes.

Reid (2012) argues that test results cannot become the basis for major educational reforms, with a common tactic being the adoption of policies from countries at the top of the league tables. Contextual differences make this problematic. Other solutions commonly include retorts to suggestions of greater school autonomy, reforming teacher education programs, or increasing competition among schools.

However, as argued in the preceding chapter, equating "quality" (never formally defined), with high rankings and test scores determined by narrowly targeted instruments is a misguided exercise that ignores the majority of students' learning pursuits, teachers' assessments and the majority of offerings delivered by education institutions. And when standards stay the same or drop slightly, teachers are blamed. Eggers & Clements Calegari (2011) argue:

> When we don't get the results we want in our military endeavors, we dont blame the soldiers. . . . No, if the results aren't there, we blame the planners. We blame the generals, the secretary of defense, the Joint Chiefs of Staff. No one contemplates blaming the men and women fighting every day in the trenches for little pay and scant recognition.
>
> And yet in education we do just that. When we don't like the way our students score on international standardized tests, we blame the teachers. When we don't like the way particular schools perform, we blame the teachers and restrict their resources.

Apple (in Hayes, Mills, Christie & Lingard, 2006, p. v) argues that, rather than focusing on whether students are successful in excellence metrics, educators should interrogate underlying assumptions and purposes by asking:

- Whose knowledge is this and how did it become "official"?
- What counts as "standards," who should decide them, and how should they be used?
- What is the relationship between this knowledge and people who have the cultural, social, and economic capital in this society?
- Whose interests does this knowledge serve; who does not benefit from current definitions of legitimate knowledge?
- What can teachers do to change to more just curricula and pedagogies?

Piety (2013), however, believes the educational data movement has many benefits and will stay, yet even the U.S. Department of Education (2009) evidence suggests that the link between testing and improvements in student learning achievement is inconclusive (in Piety, 2013). In light of "new-world" technologies and the changes they will spawn, standardized testing, didactic teaching styles, inflexible, conventional age-based progression through schooling, 40-minute lesson timetabling, traditional education calendars, bell-curve assessment expectations—really miss the point (see chapter 7).

IN CONCLUSION

Policies aiming for "excellence for all" pertain to individualized programming to meet diverse learning needs, while standardization policies and practices undermine educational equity efforts through their narrow focus and powerful influence. Individuation and standardization are conflicting policy pursuits.

Chapter Seven

"New World" versus "Old World" Thinking

Ubiquitous "disruptive technologies" (Bower & Christensen, 1995) are game-changers that are altering human existence and experience. "Newworld" technologies in a global economy offer untold possibilities for every aspect of life. They create contemporary forms of interacting, socializing, communicating, thinking, and behaving across boundaries of time and space.

Exponentially advancing technologies are now changing educational leadership, business, and governance—let alone teaching and learning—in ways that are shaking up decades of traditional education practice. The disruption is increasingly difficult to navigate, presenting challenges to current thinking, practice, and policy, alongside enormous opportunities for advancement and enhancement in education.

The printing press took knowledge production and information dissemination away from the primacy of the Church and the state. So, too, newworld technological game-changers of the twenty-first century are turning the world on its head, taking knowledge production, information dissemination, and analysis away from educators and educational institutions. The Internet had its twenty-fifth anniversary in 2013. Being an enabler of globalization, it locates education and educational institutions at a junction between the old world of certainty, order, and stability and the new world of uncertainty, disorder, and disruption.

Moore's law (1965) suggests that the complexity, capacity, and speed of technology doubles every two years, and paradoxically, as power and capability rises, component prices drop. Moore's law has been proven, but the two-year timespan is continually decreasing.

In 1970, futurist Alvin Toffler coined the term "future shock" to describe the phenomenon of accelerating change along with an overwhelming sense of information overload that outstrips human ability to keep up—a situation whereby too much change occurring in too short a period of time creates psychological anxiety for individuals and entire societies. If that was the case over four decades ago, then the term is even more relevant now. New devices, software, apps, social media platforms, nomenclature, ideas, and developments come to our attention daily, portending future opportunities with huge implications.

The cell phones we carry in our pockets today are more powerful and capable than the computers (and slide rules) used to land men on the moon in 1969. Ray Kurzweil's (2005) prophecy about "singularity"—the technology/biology intersection that augments our physical lives, senses, and experiences—is almost complete. We carry or wear digital devices that provide constant access to reality and virtual reality.

Answers to every question are literally at our fingertips and tech-savvy students living hyper-connected lives are unconstrained by space, time, borders, or devices. There are even suggestions that advances in robotics, artificial intelligence, and biological enhancements are very near to challenging "what it is to be a man" (see, for example, 33rdsquare.com).

Globalization ensures that the time taken to get innovation to market and consumer take-up times are diminishing. This is a market designed "just for you" that takes the notion of market choice and sovereign individuality to extreme levels. Current-day technology enables manufacturers to move from mass production to mass customization through robot-operated production lines assembling differing goods, tailored to individual customers' specifications. Custom-made goods are breaking mass-production business models, and the same influences are evident in education (see chapter 6).

In many circumstances, the need for education campuses, office spaces, shop fronts, physical commercial premises, telephony, many resources, physical information and filing systems, face-to-face meetings, and teaching can be eliminated. New roles are foreseeable and many existing jobs will go (see for example, Schiller, 2013). Crowd-sourcing and instant messaging speed up and democratize ideas, fundraising, and innovations. We currently have mood enhancers, but within this century, we will have neural implants to augment memory, sight, hearing, and physical ability (Marcus & Koch, 2014).

Smart driverless cars operating in smart cities, Google Glass, 3-D printing and the mooted 4-D printing, D-Wave and quantum computers, bitcoin, the Lifenaut Project, ems, bots and cyborgs, the colonization of Mars, climate re-engineering, genetically engineered "Fankenfoods" and livestock, all-seeing, hearing, and spying nonobotic drones, the immortality and posthuman culture projects are a few of the seemingly sci-fi projects currently underway that will change human lives irrevocably. Education and educational institutions cannot remain unaffected.

Some new-world innovations have been incorporated and accommodated in education, but others will prove to be education game-changers of massive consequence and yet more will appear before this book is even finished.

Education policy, stuck in old-world rigid, bureaucratic, industrial control mode, often fails to pick up on new-world potential, however, and in some circumstances actively impedes it. This chapter discusses the collision of industrial era thinking with digital- and quantum-age thinking and the messy policy intersections that make difficulties for educational leadership, business, and governance.

It would be impossible to delve into every new-world game-changer in depth and ponder what it might mean for education. Here the focus is on specific developments that are already a reality and are already making their influence felt. The discussion focuses on MOOCs (massive open online courses) and the impact of emergent computing developments, as just two examples.

MOOCS

The not-for-profit Kahn Academy has been offering free, self-paced online courses, materials, resources, and assessment tools since 2008, using video lectures in a wide range of subjects and at varying education levels. This idea is taken to extremes in higher education via MOOCs that emerged in 2012. MOOCs are offered free of charge to anyone (without prerequisites), anywhere, via the Internet—and they are rapidly sweeping through the global higher education landscape.

MOOCs open up Ivy League universities and provide global accessibility to high-profile professors and researchers (Bohle, 2013). Once open for enrollments, the take-up of these self-directed courses immediately ran into the millions of users, faster than Twitter or Facebook (Lewin, 2013a). Two of the world's most well-known MOOCs, Coursera and Udacity (both developed by Stanford University professors), are for-profit education technology companies established through venture capital (Lewin, 2013a).

EdX, however, is a MOOC cofounded, funded, and run by Harvard University and the Massachusetts Institute of Technology as a part of their suite of offerings.

These large-scale, open-teaching, connected courses are instigated with various intersecting rationale: access and equity. "Education should be a right not a privilege" (Coursera inventors Koller and Ng, cited in Lewin, 2013a), including the social responsibility of the developed-world responsibility to developing countries; MOOCs are a logical step in the globalization and internationalization of education that transcends time, national borders, and ideological boundaries; and they offer business and cost efficiency.

In addition to these broad-scale impetuses, this education game-changer also addresses concerns about lectures forming the bastion of knowledge transmission in higher education, with student attendance dropping drastically, with decades of unfavorable critiques about the pedagogical effectiveness of lectures (for example, Bligh, 1998; Groves, 2012; Owens & Price, 2010), and with the expense in providing large-scale auditoria with contemporary lecture capture capacity (which ensures even fewer students attending in person).

The business model behind MOOCs might appear perplexing, however. For example, John Barker, vice chancellor and president of the University of New England in Australia, argues that while universities may be cannibalizing their own businesses through the introduction of MOOCs, that is preferable to "someone else eating my lunch" (Kelly, 2013). The courses offered cost around $50,000 to produce (with videography being the biggest cost), and they require staff to monitor discussion forums, yet they are free to students.

Revenue streams can be generated through licensing, assessment fees, fees for certificates of completion, verification of recruitment data to potential employers, kickbacks from recommended textbook sales, and getting fee-paying recruits into degree courses by offering credits for MOOC completion. Further revenues are being canvassed through advertising or sponsorships on MOOC sites and through the introduction of paid introductory and remedial courses to assist students in completing a MOOC.

New avenues of employment for third-party examiners and those helping with degree assemblage ("un-schooling counselors," according to Schiller, 2013) are foreseeable (Friedman, 2013; Schiller, 2013).

Aoun (2013) foresees private companies examining and providing credentials for MOOC completion. Traditional quality measures—based on the number of students rejected by traditional higher education institutions, for example—will be replaced by the number of students accepted. Having to pay for a tertiary qualification may be rejected by "consumers" who prefer to take offered courses for free or at low cost.

The proliferation of digital open "badges"—formal recognition of learning and skill achievement from a range of sources and contexts—demonstrates an increasing need to provide concrete evidence of educational achievement and competency. Badges issued by educational institutions and subsidiary organizations will democratize and broaden credentialing and learning recognition.

Badges come in differing sizes and have differing purposes and hierarchies: Small badges provide feedback as learning proceeds; lower level badges may be required to unlock higher order badges. Open Badge Infrastructure gauges achievement consistency, enabling the portability and verification of badges (see Mozilla, 2013).

MOOCs enable both totally online and blended or hybrid means of obtaining a degree, with coursework chosen and sourced from universities around the world (Friedman, 2013; Tapscott, 2012). Friedman (2013) argues of MOOCs:

> I can see a day soon where you'll create your own college degree by taking the best online courses from the best professors from around the world—some computing from Stanford, some entrepreneurship from Wharton, some ethics from Brandeis, some literature from Edinburgh—paying only the nominal fee for the certificates of completion. It will change teaching, learning and the pathway to employment. There is a new world unfolding and everyone will have to adapt.

Cadwalladr (2012) speaking of her experiences with MOOCs and traditional lectures agrees: "What the new websites are doing is raising questions about what a university is and what it's for. And how to pay for it." Conceding the agonies of funding mass global education amid rapid change in higher education Cadwalladr (2012) concludes: "There's no doubting that this is something of a turning point."

Discussion and opinion surrounding the introduction of MOOCs as a postindustrial, new-world teaching tool is nonconclusive. Few MOOC enrollees actually finish their courses, yet completion rates are higher when personal online help is available. Academics' unions argue that MOOCs are forcing massive workload increases, overburdening staff, creating unpaid overtime, and increasing casualization in the higher education workforce (Friedman, 2013). There are suggestions that MOOCs could render textbooks obsolete, as all course materials are posted online. And MOOCs development is costly (Bohle, 2013).

However, despite the cost of developing and staffing MOOCs, the potential forward revenue from course credits is presumed to make this short-term expenditure pay off. Proponents—many of whom are commentators with no current firsthand experience in working in universities or with MOOCs—contend that online technologies make "flipped classrooms" possible, with content material made available online, with face-to-face time spent on inquiry, problem solving, team projects, and discussion (see for example, Bastian, 2014).

Assessment of student learning in MOOCs—a major staff problem in courses with huge student numbers—is moving beyond initial automated tick-box arrangements to having assessments using considered, human judgments that pose questions and ideas to enhance learning. Marking student work is an expensive exercise so crowd-sourced peer-to-peer assessment arrangements are available (Berg, 2013). This requires guidance via specific assessment criteria and feedback advice materials, but is intended to provide a concrete purpose for assessment beyond issues about credentialing through multiple sources of feedback, while opening up networks of conversations.

Educational leaders, governors, and business officials can speculate as to the long-term effects, but as the MOOCs movement spreads rapidly across the higher education sector throughout the world, one wonders about the viability of huge infrastructure, permanent unionized staff, and timetables determined by industrial-age hours.

MOOCs serve as a clarion call for the rapid reinvention of higher education institutions, with emphasis on innovative approaches to teaching and learning (Bokor, 2012; Dane, 2013). Coursera financier Scott Sandell argues:

> Monetization is not the most important objective for this business at this point. What is important is that Coursera is rapidly accumulating a body of high-quality content that could be very attractive to universities that want to license it for their own use. We invest with a very long mind-set, and the gestation period of the very best companies is at least 10 years. (Cited in Lewin, 2013a)

MOOCs assemble course units from many universities onto one digital platform that can be accessed by anyone, anywhere, at any time. This solves a problem with access and class- and race-based hierarchies, but portends the kind of foundational disruption to universities as has occurred with traditional storefront retailing, banking, and communication companies: "the end of higher education as we know it" (Aoun 2013, p. 1). New competitors in the marketplace will provide the same services, curtailing the monopoly currently enjoyed by traditional universities.

Aoun (2013) foresees the possibility of high-cost, "luxury," on-campus universities competing with low-cost, "economy," virtual courses, thereby exacerbating rather than ameliorating equity differentials. He summarizes: "Whether the MOOC phenomenon becomes a boon or a bane to higher education remains to be seen. But one thing is certain: It will change higher education forever." Diaz (in Wuorio, 2012) agrees, arguing that "education as a whole will see more change in the next 10 years than in the previous 50."

One may wonder, however, about the feasibility of courses requiring laboratory or workplace practical experiences (such as teaching) and whether virtual reality can capture this space to enable adequate education within particular professions.

While internationalization, equity, cost, and profit motives remain imminent issues at all levels and sectors of education, it would not be surprising to see a replication of higher education's MOOCs happening at the school level and in the training sector.

GENIUS MACHINES AND UBIQUITOUS VIRTUAL REALITY

Google Glass, released in 2014, will be the first broadly used hands-free multifunction Internet device. Google Glass responds to a wearer's audible requests and is worn like a pair of eyeglasses with its small "glass" high over one eye, so avoiding obstruction to usual sightlines. Google Glass answers questions in text, it translates words and sentences into various languages, provides directions, delivers ahead-of-time information relating to imminent schedules, takes pictures and videos, and shares lived actuality—what is actually being seen and experienced—with nonpresent others in real time.

At the time of writing, Google Glass has just been released, with global demands expected to rival the advent of smart phones and iPads. Take-up will no doubt be as rapid as the future improved versions of what will become a must-have device. What will it mean when students have simultaneous access to both the virtual world and reality? What will this mean for many resources we rely on in education—including libraries and resource centers?

And first generation quantum computers are emerging, based on quantum mechanics with such enormous capacity, speed, and power that they challenge human intelligence as they solve problems in seconds that would require eons through conventional computers. In quantum computers qubits replace silicon chips and transisters. (Qubits are electrical circuits that behave like magnets and interact with each other in nonlinear ways to enable almost immediate availability of solutions and information. They use quantum algorithms rather than the current probabilistic algorithms.)

The developers of D-Wave technology admit that it is difficult to imagine how quantum computers or "genius machines" will be used or what their effects will be, but there is no doubting the impact will be astonishing and inconceivable in terms of current understandings about the world. And what will they mean for education?

The notion of individuation or individualized education programming was a topic discussed in chapter 6. New-world technologies will make customization even more achievable. The next generation of computers will be much more intuitive, with apps contextualized to the person and the context in which she or he lives and works.

To make the next generation web services even more lifelike and realistic, inventors will go back to basics so that Internet usage will be much more akin to having a face-to-face conversation. The computer will intuitively determine the context in which the information is required, what the person it's interacting with is thinking, trying to do and say and make appropriate responses. To accomplish this, the real-life context of the user will be aggregated and analyzed. The device will account for PAGE: persona (personality), affinity (likes and dislikes), goals (what the user wants to achieve or accomplish), and environment (the physical location and time in which the interaction occurs).

But it doesn't finish there. Aspects such as agendas and past conversations or interactions are taken into account on top of the most important feature (in my mind), an authentic, satisfying user experience (unlike the frustratingly clunky and user-unfriendly experiences we've all had in our online lives). Having apps that intuit so completely, so ubiquitously, and omnisciently seems to be both too good to be true and a little unnerving (after all, the computer will know everything about us). Davie (2013, p. 1) says:

> Data analysis of user behavior makes mass personalization and behavioral segmentation possible. Who a user is, where they are, what they are trying to accomplish, and the type of device they're using all matter. The result: The next generation of the web will be driven by context.

In the future, some believe, genetics will be the basis for remediation to achieve equity in education, made possible via advanced technologies. Asbury, Gladwell & Goldin (2013) argue there is evidence that educational ability is influenced by the genes we inherit, affecting reading and mathematical ability and influencing how easy or difficult it is for an individual to acquire new learning. This goes beyond the learning experience or the environment in which learning takes place.

This discovery will almost certainly influence the connections between learning outcomes and the teaching methods employed to achieve them (see Kendall [with Asbury, Gladwell & Goldin], 2013), including increasing momentum in individualizing the curriculum and pedagogy.

THE DOWNSIDES OF DISRUPTIVE TECHNOLOGIES

The amazing capabilities and possibilities brought to us through technologies also have their downsides. No information is secure or private. If signing up to a social media or information service is free, it is the user who is the product. Personal accounts enable the provider and myriad other businesses to profit and grow via the information provided. Privacy and data security are enormous new realms of risk to be managed alongside numerous economic and legal issues. Spying on consumers is the other side of the economics of privacy (see for example, Angwin, 2010).

As an example, Hesse (2010) reports that just as it's possible to measure the age of trees through their bark rings, so could moving from MySpace, Facebook, and Gowalla, but stopping before Formspring, be a giveaway of age. Millennials aged eighteen to twenty-four are the most likely group to experience identity theft, since their life statistics, activities, location, and interests are available online (Klein, 2010). And cyber-bullying is a new area of education policy formation.

Behind social media giants are silent bots that come across as "friends" at first before switching to monitor and "surveil" their hosts for social research purposes—to categorize and group, to advertise and promote products, to proliferate messages, friends lists or, for more devious purposes including embezzlement and blackmail.

Mobile devices with GPS pinpoint user location make personalized, locally specific advertising or campaigning easy. As you drive past your local school, a political campaigner can send you a message spruiking a political party's spending on the school's upgrade, or damning another party for their neglect or mismanagement of improvements. While consumers have rights to privacy, some will value their privacy sufficiently highly to pay for heightened information protection (Druschel, Backes & Tirtea, 2012).

Having continuous connectivity to information may produce nimble, adaptive, multitasking, rapidly responsive individuals, but the downside to "always-on" tech-savvy lifestyles may be impatience, a propensity for quick fixes, instant gratification, and a disinclination toward considered decision making or deep thinking (Anderson & Rainie, 2012).

Will we tire of these innovations, invitations to join a network, or other people's endless posts, many of which are sheer time wasters? Who can keep up and still have a life—on Tumblr, Gowalla, Foursquare, Posterous, Quantcast, Friendster, Fromspring, Quora.com, Hunch.com, let alone Facebook and Twitter? Is there a saturation point when people can't see the point, don't want to waste their time, don't have the inclination to participate in social media, and say, "enough is enough"? (Hesse, 2010). Current experience suggests not.

In advanced countries, technology is a major eater of resources, an essential means by which teaching and learning occur and through which the organization can operate and function in every imaginable way. We simply cannot do without computers and an increasing range of apps and software, let alone other technologies. We are hooked, yet education developments for computers have hardly kept pace with standards expected in other sectors, such as banking and retail. Everyone could cite a thousand examples of frustrating tech failures or security breaches that waste time, create stress, and reduce personal and organizational productivity (see chapter 3).

Educational institutions rely increasingly on online or blended modes of course delivery. However, surveys of students' learning experiences and research into staff usage and competence in technological applications signal considerable slippage between intentions and actuality. For example, Starr, Stacey and Grace (2011) and Starr (2012c) found that a large amount of self-motivation and personal interest in technology is required for academics to be as confident and effective as possible in online teaching, but this can't be guaranteed.

Among other things, major concerns are inadequate provision and access to professional learning and little in the way of personalized one-on-one assistance. This lack, topped with an expectation that keeping up-to-date and on top of new developments is a personal matter, simply leaves some staff members behind and feeling inadequate, despite their innate teaching or learning abilities. Hence, besides the enormous costs of hardware, software, and continual updates, there are costs associated with teaching the users.

Equally, there are assumptions that students can and will have access to and use interactive learning management systems effectively in order to undertake their coursework and enhance their learning.

IN CONCLUSION

The possibilities of George Orwell's *1984* (1949) and the 1970 film *The Rise and Rise of Michael Rimmer* could resemble current reality. In *1984*, the surveillant, Big Brother, watches everyone while "the truth" is controlled by the powerful. In the case of *The Rise and Rise of Michael Rimmer*, social media enables instant participatory democracy with citizens voting daily on political matters until this incessancy leads to one more vote, with a majority yes vote meaning they would never have to vote on any matter ever again.

How will the game play out? Each of the new-world developments discussed above will have a huge impact, let alone the many others that will no doubt come along and be equally or more disruptive and game-changing. But education policy, practice, and professional learning—which are equally important and huge areas individually and together—are lagging behind technological developments that are already upon us or imminent. However, some suggest that technology will never replace the teacher:

> If future models of learning means encouraging young people to spend prolonged periods in front of faceless computer screens, exposed to largely unregulated material in an inherently unsafe environment, then that is clearly not the way forward.

And:

> Good teachers have the skills to know exactly how to get the best out of each and every young person in their care. . . .
> No "new models of learning" can ever compromise or threaten the essence of what a teacher is, always has been and always will be. (Wright, 2013, p. 1)

Others are not so sure as new technologies are escaping the screen.

Education policy and practice have been slow to catch on to the implications of technological developments, but there is awareness that things can't and won't stay the same (*The Economist*, 2013a). Currently too little thought or attention is paid to disruptive technologies until their take-up is increasing and the technologies are unable to be ignored. In the meantime, the old world has much at threat, but it is not dead. Old hierarchies, inequities, continual emphases on standardization and measurement, and a reliance on falling back on what's been "tried and true" show few signs of being repealed.

It is time for some deep thinking, massive change, and new understandings to come to the fore.

Chapter Eight

Sustainability versus Growth

At present, we are stealing the future, selling it in the present, and calling it GDP.
—Paul Hawken

Educational institutions react to policy effects at the micro (institutional) level created by decisions made at macro (federal/national) and meso (state or district) levels. Effects include curriculum change, budget cuts, institutional closures, increased class sizes, or program reductions or discontinuation (see for example, Bohn, Reyes & Johnson, 2013; Dillon, 2008; Lytton, 2011).

For a long time, but especially since the global financial crisis of 2008 and subsequent recession, budgetary constraints have added to education business concerns and have produced specific policy responses. They have been the impetus for extracting value for money, cranking up cost efficiencies and increasing demands for raised productivity to support economic growth.

As discussed in earlier chapters, governments have positioned education as a major means of ensuring economic competitiveness, productivity, growth, and higher returns in a global economy. And as has also been discussed previously, the ways in which education policy is tamed to comply with economic goals can impede, rather than encourage, policy aims. The straitjacketed, QED (*quod erat demonstrandum*), technically obsessive ways in which education policy has demanded greater accountability, doing more with less, have taken focus and energy away from teaching, learning, and research.

Along with policy activities motivated by economic imperatives, however, are calls for education institutions to be sustainable. Expectations are that they will support and promote green, energy-efficient operations to save precious resources and reduce waste while encouraging attitudinal and behavioral changes for a sustainable global future. Sustainability in education comprises both education programs and environmentally friendly institutional practices (see for example, Sustainability Victoria, 2014).

UNESCO argues that the notion of sustainability is "a process of change in relationships between social, economic, and natural systems and processes" (1997, p. 13). In keeping with this suggestion, the ways in which the word "sustainability" is currently being used in education has broadened to include the sustainability of people, communities, and cultures, as well as the stewardship of education institutions and programs (see for example, Bottery, 2011, 2012).

Environmental sustainability and ecological protection are now seen to go hand in hand with concerns about human health and issues such as economic equity, social justice, and work-life balance, and on all these fronts, education plays an important and pivotal role. Hence, educational leaders, business managers, and governors must also consider their community responsibilities (with every community having differing concerns and issues) and the corporate social responsibility or ethicality of their suppliers and community partners. (Health and well-being concerns are related to these recent considerations, and are discussed in chapter 9.)

Education for sustainability concerns educating the young to cope with realities confronting the fragile and perilous world they are inheriting with its interconnected political, economic, social, cultural, and environmental problems.

Many scientists and commentators argue that we have gone past the point of no return in terms of climate change (Hamilton, 2010; Suzuki, 2013)—that as a species we have reached the anthropocene—a new geological epoch ("Anthropocene" is a term coined by Iowa State University biology professor Eugene Stoermer and popularized by Nobel Prize winning climate scientist, Paul Crutzen [2006] to refer to massive extinction and ecological damage due to human causes).

The world "is in mortal danger," argues Beare (2010, p. 18), while Rees (2003) predicts that the world is being so overburdened and exploited that it will not survive past this current century. Suzuki (2013) argues that the only answer is to adapt and dramatically change our lifestyles—a task in which educational authorities must play a large part. Sequestering carbon, managing biodiversity, and growing food more intensively to feed a growing world have become mainstream concerns.

EMERGING PRACTICES

As components of the learning program, education for sustainability and environmental education are increasingly popular pursuits. Educational institutions around the developed world are being encouraged to "embed sustainability in everything they do" (Sustainability Victoria, 2014), although take-up has been slower than many would like to see.

The UK government wants every school to be sustainable by 2020; Australian governments (federal and state partnerships) have developed the Australian Sustainable Schools Initiative to internalize a culture of sustainability (Trainor, 2012). Benefits include cost reductions but go far beyond this: Sustainability concerns all members of the population; it endorses a message of reducing consumption and living with less.

Education for sustainable development aims to endow students with the capabilities to solve complex and competing social, economic, and environmental issues so as to ensure the sustainability of the planet (UNESCO, 1997, 2007). Lasting change occurs as individuals make behavioral and attitudinal changes through critical inquiry and concern; and educational institutions can become leadership hubs for learning for sustainability.

Programs for healthy sustainable lifestyles are emerging at all levels of education. In the early years, primary and secondary school kitchen garden programs are proliferating (see for example, Kitchen Garden Foundation, 2014). Water collection and conservation, recycling, energy saving programs, biodiversity promotion, and greenhouse gas emissions reduction programs are widespread (see for example, Cutter-MacKenzie, 2010b). ICT (information and communications technology), life extension, and refresh and recycling programs are actively encouraged (see for example, Victorian Auditor-General, 2012). New buildings must be energy efficient.

"Prosumption" is promoted—as opposed to consumption—with educators and education institutions swapping, jointly purchasing, sharing, and recycling assets and services. Although this may be the antithesis of what economists may prescribe to stimulate economic growth in stagnant economies, these moves disrupt patterns of continual growth, waste, greed, and the emptiness and excesses of individualism and hyper-consumption.

As Botsman and Rogers (2010) explain, collaborative consumerism utilizes technology, social networking, and crowd power to engender and encourage collaborative consumer behaviors and greater collective trust in getting what is needed to where it is needed, when it is needed. This movement comprises a redistributive market through:

- recirculating used and unwanted goods to those who need and want them, through trading or donations;
- reusing, reducing, recycling, and repairing existing goods;

- collaborative lifestyles, sharing money (social lending), skills, and time;
- product service systems whereby goods can be used to a maximal extent through renting or shared ownership (owning seldom-used goods outright no longer makes sense); and
- forming free-labor groups for a common purpose—collective, community action to achieve the greening or cleaning of campuses, for example (Anderson, 2010).

In many of these schemes, no money changes hands, and if it does, costs associated with middlemen are eliminated. Equipment, services, personnel, governance, finances, and intellectual property—can all be shared, borrowed, collectively owned, rented, or loaned for the good of all parties. Possibilities are endless, with necessity being the mother of invention.

There is evidence of the return of the educational institution that is owned by the community (Engelhardt & Engelhardt, 1940), offering education to students during the day and facilities for adult/community education, recreation, and other civic purposes during nonschool hours (although any educational institution funded by the public can be used for civic as well as educational purposes). Community schools save enormous expenditures of public funds on infrastructure and ensure facilities are used at all times, rather than laying idle during evenings, weekends, and holidays. This idea makes increasing sense over the seventy years since Engelhardt and Engelhardt suggested it in the 1940s.

There is justification in the view that "[n]o public [education institution] should be developed which does not have a community relationship" and that "buildings may become less monumental but better places for the inculcation and practice of democratic principles" (p. ix). The call for a "better coordination among the services organized to meet community needs" (p. viii) to avoid expensive duplication, exclusion, and segregation appears to be validated.

The Engelhardts believed that community schools would share their social recreation spaces; cafeteria and commercial kitchens; auditoria; arts creation, performance and exhibition spaces; study, staff, and meeting rooms; the library/resource center; counseling and guidance facilities; vocational learning spaces; medical facilities; and sports grounds, parks, and gardens.

These arrangements concur with moves toward closer community partnerships and cross-sector/cross-level alliances. Several school complexes in Australia are jointly owned and operated by the three schooling sectors: government, Catholic, and independent. They share recreation space and specialist facilities, and, increasingly, teachers work across schools, while cooperating in shared curriculum programs.

The underlying rationale is compelling and makes sense on a number of levels: financial, social, and community building and cohesion, without unnecessary duplication, enabling a more thorough and comprehensive range of services and facilities. Cooperation is all that is required.

There is growing encouragement for telecommuting—working from home—to relieve pressures on parking lots, office space, and utilities costs. This is often a popular option for staff and is a growing trend, which places further questions around the sustainability of current infrastructure, employment practices, and *modus operandi*.

There are suggestions that governments should introduce product-stewardship legislation so that companies creating waste and pollution through manufacturing processes are responsible for reducing, removing, or neutralizing resultant waste. These would become new accountabilities to communities.

And social commentator Hugh Mackay (2013) suggests that we start to look after each other by promoting a sense of charity and openheartedness in the home. The term "kith and kin" once referred to responsibilities for looking after relatives, our home environments, and communities. Similarly, the saying "charity begins at home" once had a very different meaning than that ascribed to it today.

The contemporary assumption is that this saying suggests taking care of our own at home—meaning in our own domicile, community, or country—before providing aid to others further afield. But the saying originally referred to the role of the home in developing instincts to be charitable. In other words, a sense of charity and kindness toward others is an honorable trait that should be instilled in children by familial adults.

Mackay (2013) believes the original interpretation should be reinculcated, to make for a more caring world—toward each other, other species, and our planet. In other words, charity and sharing should be part of education from an early age.

BARRIERS AND PARADOX

Sustainability pursuits compete with the economic growth imperatives of governments and corporations. Barriers to sustainability concern the mixed messages received from media advertising and governmental economic stimulus packages promoting spending, growth, and consumerism.

Education is seen to play a large role in both camps: Politicians and corporate moguls see education as a means to achieve economic growth and improve GDP, innovation, and productivity, while environmentalists, health, well-being, and sustainability proponents see education in terms of embedding changes for good that run counter to the prevailing culture of consumerism and growth.

Sustainability pursuits in education exist in an age of hyper-materialism, when the consumers of education have very high expectations about the services and resources they will encounter. Facilities such as student parking lots are now commonplace (and in some instances, the cars in the high school students' lot are better than those belonging to staff); technology requires constant updating, and there is more attention given to the appearance and upkeep of campuses, especially the size and extent of the built environment.

Educational institutions are more into consumerism and materialism than ever before. And decisions around these activities probably occur with too little regard for the environmental impact behind the manufacture or arrival of education purchases. Certainly, the expanding demands of consumers place extreme pressure on budgets that have to accommodate increasing considerations.

Barriers to sustainability in education are also reported to be a lack of finances, uncommitted leadership, insufficient incentives, and low community demand on top of the sheer fact that educational leaders, business managers, and governors are simply too overwhelmed with other day-to-day issues to engage fully with sustainability issues (Wright & Horst, 2013). Underestimated are the enormous complexity of day-to-day activities and interactions in educational institutions (Bottery, 2012).

Suzuki (2013) refers to willful blindness, as economic growth takes priority above everything else, with nature and the environment being shoehorned into economic agendas. (Illustrating this point is the United Nations Copenhagen Climate Change Conference of 2009. Despite its having delegates from 192 countries and long deliberations, no agreement about climate change action and no legally binding resolutions were accomplished.)

At some point, however, motivations toward both economic growth and sustainability intersect: For example, conserving energy saves money; finding efficient ways to conduct business saves time and effort; providing opportunities for students to learn about sustainability provides tangible community and individual benefits (Cutter-MacKenzie, 2010a). Yet these colossal and grave issues are also inherently contradictory and paradoxical. At many junctures these impetuses work against and frustrate the aims of the other. Educational leaders, business managers, and governors have to do their best to accommodate all policy agendas.

Although sustainability is gaining traction in education in general, understandings about sustainability and the role of educators are inconsistent, and ideas about how sustainable development might be achieved differ enormously (Wright & Horst, 2013).

Paradoxically, government and education policies have a foot in both growth and sustainability camps. There is a disconnect between political agendas and many segments of the community, and as far as environmental stewardship is concerned, with political policy agendas focused on the short term, political leaders are failing in their leadership responsibilities.

Chapter 9 discusses how these two contradictory pressures of sustainability and growth play out from the human perspective.

Chapter Nine

Work-Life Balance versus Work Intensification

It is no measure of health to be well-adjusted to a profoundly sick society.
—Jiddu Krishnamurti

Modern methods of production have given us the possibility of ease and security for all; we have chosen, instead, to have overwork for some and starvation for others. Hitherto we have continued to be as energetic as we were before there were machines; in this we have been foolish, but there is no reason to go on being foolish forever.
—Bertrand Russell

The preceding chapters discuss the numerous implications and effects of economic imperatives in education policy, including the policy accouterments of efficiency, productivity, and accountability. Policy expectations exhort that educational institutions must become more autonomous, self-reliant, and responsible; raise standards and improve student outcomes—especially measurable outcomes—while adapting to greater cost efficiencies cutbacks and market competition.

"Doing more with less" is the new bottom line, but demands go beyond the core business of teaching and learning to include numerous elements that were once alien to the educational environment (see for example, Gard, 2013).

This chapter concentrates on the professional, personal, and corporeal effects of such a policy culture and practice demands on the educational workforce. It advances the conversation about pressures for growth and sustainability, efficiency, and productivity, by examining the effects on so-called human resources.

It is assumed that people are an organization's most precious assets, with effective personnel being pivotal to the entire enterprise, institutional reputation, and outcomes. However, the ability to save time and labor through technology, pressures for growth, increased productivity, and continuous improvement, have resulted in the intensification and 24/7 nature of educational work and continual function creep in education roles, in order to ensure that a rising numbers of tasks are met. Ironically, this may mean that they cannot be executed to exacting standards (despite widespread policy discourses promoting "excellence").

In a dynamic policy environment, personnel have to be agile, adaptable, and flexible to cope with continual change and uncertainty. To a large extent, education survives on the goodwill of its employees in contexts where funds are always in limited supply and where people work above and beyond the call of duty to ensure educational institutions run as smoothly as possible. When funding is stretched, however, the shortfall is often stemmed by cuts to staffing, resourcing, or service budgets, with growing instances of redundancies and the nonrenewal of employment contracts to make ends meet.

The rationale behind education policies that lead to work intensification are many and the problems that politicians and economists are trying to solve are obvious. To use an Australian example, in response to slowdown in growth of national income, Australia's Productivity Commission (2013) recommends actions such as increasing taxation, improving efficiency and productivity in the education and health sectors, and raising the pension age to seventy.

Current economic growth rates are purportedly unsustainable to the extent that the nation is sitting on a "time bomb" (see for example, Tingle, 2014). Aging populations will add around 6 percent to gross domestic product by mid-century. To cope with rising budgetary pressures occurring through education expenses during the first decades of individuals' lives and health and old-age pensions and aged-care costs during the latter decades, economists are advising swift, appropriate but uncomfortable public policy interventions, or, they warn, looming problems will worsen.

Governments aim to expand the job market, grow the economy, and reduce social policy expenditure while maintaining high standards of living. These aims are reprioritizing traditional areas of government spending. Both governments and the business sector are demanding a flexible, deregulated workforce, while policy also has the role of creating complementary psychological incentives for work, productivity, and economic competitiveness. The "age of entitlement" is over.

Ironically, it is in this no-frills, cost-cutting, lean but increased-output context that educational institutions are implementing work-life balance policies, encouraging staff to take their leave entitlements (to reduce leave liability), to be mindful of their health and well-being needs, while clamoring for recognition through "employer of choice" citations.

Adding to this paradox are growing numbers of stress-related sick leave and compensation claims and greater dissatisfaction among education workers about unwelcomed, extraordinary, or unfamiliar add-ons to their regular education-related tasks (see for example, Brown, Ralph & Brember, 2002; Carr, 1993; Gold & Roth, 2013; Mannheim, 2013; Tytherleigh, Webb, Cooper & Ricketts, 2005: Van der Doef & Maes, 1999). It is interesting to note that stress claims have increased dramatically over the years of restructuring in education, despite tightened definitions of eligibility for compensation (see for example, Mannheim, 2013).

"Work-life balance" and "well-being" are increasingly heard terms, which are seen as positives that must be taken more seriously—including inculcating sensible working hours and moratoria on expected excesses of unpaid overtime that are part of a culture perceived as greedy, antisocial, immoral, and unethical (Franzway, 2001). All work and no play is a dismal state of affairs for professional workers.

WORK INTENSIFICATION

Much has been written about the effects of increasing work expectations without extra time or money to complete or compensate for extra tasks—referred to as "work intensification"—or working longer hours, including unpaid hours of work, as a result of doing more with less.

An expanding, constantly changing, and often conflicting policy environment has increased workloads, with educators and educational leaders working increasing unpaid hours at work simply to keep up (see for example, Simos, 2013).

When Bunting (2005) set up a website called "Working Lives" to collect data for her book *Willing Slaves*, she was inundated with responses. The recurrent theme was "the sheer invasive dominance of work in people's lives, and the price it exacted on their health and happiness" (Bunting, 2005, p. xiii). Bunting's respondents cited feeling "owned," always "on call," with long hours and hard work never being "quite enough," while life had become something to be "endured rather than enjoyed."

Work demands, in many instances and increasingly, exceed the capacity of individuals to cope (Bunting, 2005). Toffler's (1970) "future shock" is reality, although his prediction that technological change would eventuate in increased leisure is not. From an educational context—in this case the schooling sector—Gard's (2013) observations sum up the situation:

> If you speak to the principal of just about any . . . school, chances are they'll tell you two things about the changes they've seen in the past couple of

decades. First, they'll mention increasing pressure to improve test scores in the narrowly traditional areas of the curriculum, most obviously literacy and numeracy.

But they'll also tell you about the paperwork and increasing policies for which they are accountable: bullying, sex education, child protection, skin cancer, alcohol, drugs, nutrition, obesity and mental health.

Educational institutions are being asked to do more when they have less time to devote to "noncore" activities. With increasing controls and accountabilities, cumulative and intensified work, public criticism, and blame, there is less time, space, and perhaps inclination for change. Reform fatigue and work overload are a result. One educational leader interviewed in this research during the first fortnight of the academic year stated "everyone is worn out already."

Hartley (2013) suggests that productivity agendas have changed the nature of academic work that was once more social, with lunch and coffee breaks taken in a communal space with colleagues. These times are long gone. Although these activities ensure that individuals are refreshed and promote the sharing of ideas, problem solving, and information in the natural course of a day, these activities are now viewed as time wasting. Academics argue that work now entails considerable time sitting at computers. Increased workload pressures entail "locking oneself" away from common or social areas (or interferences).

For example, increasing numbers of academics are submitting articles to editors of academic refereed journals on weekends and public holidays, including Christmas Day, demonstrating long working hours even when on holidays (Cabanac & Hartley, 2013; Ladle, Malhado & Todd, 2007). The publish-or-perish creed, expanded extra-curricular duties, and administrative function creep contribute to such work intensification.

Atomistic work patterns enabled by technological innovations and 24/7 accessibility make it difficult to retreat from work. Recognizing that workers are "on deck" at places and times outside the office and usual working hours, many educational institutions, especially universities, are encouraging telecommuting, or working from home, to improve productivity, to alleviate pressures on parking lots (resource efficiencies), and to reduce the necessity of one-office-per-person arrangements, while also having environmental benefits. Meanwhile students working online expect speedier responsiveness.

The disadvantages are that working anywhere and at any time means that work and private lives are constantly melded together, with no distinct personal time (see for example, Gunter, 2012; White, 2012). It is work that encroaches on unpaid, personal time, not vice versa.

An Australian example concerns the Labour Day public holiday celebrating the establishment of the internationally agreed forty-hour paid working week and the acceptance of the "8-hours of work, 8-hours of play, and 8-hours of rest" principle for a healthy society. Ironically, Australian higher education institutions do not acknowledge this public holiday—it is a regular workday. And while being paid for a 36.5-hour week, the great majority of education workers toil for up to double these hours—for no extra pay, just to cope with workload demands (Hil, 2012). This might be considered a form of poverty defined by time rather than money

In the view of Goodin, Rice, Parpo and Eriksson (2008), time is a universal good and inherently egalitarian, as it is distributed to everyone equally. Time is intrinsically scarce, since demand always outstrips supply (everyone would like more time). Those who have more discretionary time are viewed as having "more time" than others. The fact is, however, that these lucky individuals have fewer constraints, more "temporal autonomy" and discretionary control over time and, therefore, over their lives.

Individuals whose time is constrained and controlled may be viewed as victims, since their destinies are regulated by external agencies (see for example, Schor, 1992). Pryor (2008) refers to this as "doing time." Goodin et al. (2008) refer to the "time bind"—and to the busy-ness that comes about through employees' lack of control of over how busy they are, resulting in overwork and little discretionary autonomy.

The hourly rate of pay in education is pitifully low, especially if calculated as it should be: that is, with the weekly rate divided by the hours worked, and this is in a "profession" that some argue is already underpaid (Dodd, 2014; Eggers & Clements Calegari, 2011; Milburn, 2012; cf. Meyer, 2011). (Something is definitely wrong when the unqualified teenager coming to do some gardening demands a higher hourly rate than a university research fellow with a PhD who is unable to obtain permanent employment.) Are educational workers simply stupid "achievaholic nerds" and "workaholic professionals" (Pryor, 2008)?

Education as it is currently pursued, contributes to such controlling, workaholic tendencies with its structured rewards, risk aversion, and expectations of long hours for success, which gives pause for serious thought. Education, bound by economistic policies, is complicit in producing negative corporeal effects for its workforce.

A further Australian example explains the work intensification phenomenon. Australian workers purportedly work the longest hours in the Western world, contributing an estimated $72-billion gift to their employers in the form of unpaid overtime—an amount that exceeds their annual leave entitlements (The Australia Institute, 2013). In one year Australians work 2.14 billion hours of unpaid overtime, which equates to three times more than national-average volunteer labor statistics. Although workers achieved reductions in working hours early in the twentieth century, since the 1980s working hours have been steadily increasing. It is now more common to work unpaid overtime than it is to be paid for overtime. Forty-five percent of Australian workers—or more than half of fulltime employees—work more hours than they are paid for. Mostly these are white-collar workers, with expectations of unpaid work increasing the higher the remuneration as an issue of "professionalism."

The most common reason given for working unpaid overtime is that without doing so, the work would pile up, creating stress and mayhem, or the work simply would not get done. In other words, there is more work to do than is possible for one worker to complete within paid working hours. This seems incredible when every developed nation has unemployed and underemployed workers. If unpaid overtime hours were to be changed to paying positions, the Australian labor force would increase by 1.16 million workers (see Goodin et al., 2008, and Pryor, 2008). The unpaid work of $72 billion equates to 6 percent of GDP.

Unpaid overtime reduces the amount of time that workers have to spend with their families, can have negative physical- and mental-health effects, and is deleterious to child-rearing and the nation's cultural life and civil society (Bunting, 2005).

Many education workers, especially educational leaders, feel overwhelmed and exhausted by their jobs, with productivity demands triumphing over personhood and lifestyle issues (for example, Department of Education and Training, 2004; Gronn & Lacey, 2004). Educators complain that work intensification means they see less of their own children and are not the parents they would choose to be, had they sufficient time. Volunteering for community-based activities is out of the question and lives become more socially disconnected and detached (Burke & Cooper, 2008; Green, 2008).

Fear and Denniss (2013) argue that calls for productivity increases have, for too long, been a one-way street in favor of employers. They argue for reforms to ensure that workers can work reasonable hours without fear of losing their jobs, experiencing negative health effects, or sacrificing their relationships and family life. It's time, the authors claim, for massive change within workplace cultures.

Education employees, too, wonder how much more productivity can be extracted from their work in lean, intensified, DIY, education work contexts, with much existing work already going unpaid. For example, recent research in the higher education sector found that while employees are paid to work 36.5 hours per week, 85 percent worked beyond their employment hours, with 49 percent working over 50 hours and up to 80 hours per week (Starr & Toffoletti, 2010). Impacts were profound. Respondents found that work created pressures:

- in managing family life and home duties;
- in having adequate personal (nonwork) time;

- in maintaining friendships;
- in having to work in the evenings, during weekends, and while on leave;
- not taking time for lunch and coffee breaks at work;
- making work very individualistic and atomistic, as socializing meant even less time for personal activities;
- in never feeling that any one task is completed thoroughly or well enough; and
- in meeting expectations that professionals will not be time counters, despite their personal circumstances.

Education work is boundless, much of it is invisible to those who are not involved, and pressures from 360-degree stakeholders (students, parents, colleagues and systemic and regulatory authorities) add to work intensification. Now commonplace 24/7 working habits make it possible to have education and the business of education occurring outside regular hours. The research found that educators believed that to be successful in their jobs, they had to accept and persevere with working long hours.

IMPACT

Stress levels among educators are rising. Of particular concern are impacts on personal health, well-being, fitness, and happiness stemming from government policy demands, constant restructuring, rapid educational change, and exclusion from decision making (see for example, Brown et al., 2002). Job commitment and satisfaction are closely connected with levels of workplace stress (Tytherleigh et al., 2005).

Educators overwhelmingly report having too little time for exercise, getting too little sleep, feeling stressed and anxious worrying about the job, and having no time for interests outside of work, with many experiencing lifestyle illnesses (Brown et al., 2002; Gold & Roth, 2013).

Notions of work-life balance are a ruse and infeasible, given "unrealistic" expectations about work output. Payouts for psychological injury are continually rising. Overwork, bullying, management issues, work-based conflict, difficult students, demanding parents, and competitive work colleagues are cited as the major triggers (see for example, Chilcott, 2013; Makin, Cooper & Cox, 1996).

Educational leadership has been constructed in such a way that it is no longer a career—many leaders predict their jobs will become increasingly limited as a result of their short-term employment contracts, job dissatisfaction and exhaustion, and values inimicality and as ageing workers become devalued for younger tech-savvy talent.

Maslach (1982; 1999) uses the word "burnout" to describe a syndrome that is particularly prevalent in the helping professions. The definition of burnout includes initial exhaustion and stress, followed by increasing cynicism or negative reactions, followed by increasingly negative beliefs about the self in the job, such as loss of confidence and self-blame.

Maslach's (1999) conclusions about overwork, sleep deprivation, and lack of control suggest that they are not an individual problem, but an organizational one. In other words, if statistics of stress, sick leave, and burnout increase, an organizational rather than individual adjustment is required.

Overcoming burnout within organizations requires attention to issues such as sensible workload and deadline expectations; curtailing constant changes to work responsibilities and roles; greater rewards and recognition systems; a focus on creativity; and values of appreciation, fairness, and participatory decision making, so that burnout becomes superseded with engagement (Maslach, 1999).

From interviewees' accounts, work intensification is rarely taken into account by employing bodies. Rather, operating budgets have been constantly cut with concomitant workforce reductions but with no commensurate reduction in workload. Change has been constant and incessant, and comments suggest that work expectations have been unrealistic while offering little praise or recognition.

Carr (1993) suggests that the cause of much stress identified by educational leaders is the conflict between their role as an educational leader and their role as a manager. The conflict emerges from feelings of being insufficiently skilled in managerial and business tasks, from feeling that these tasks are compromised or stand in opposition to their values in education. In addition, educational leaders report losing control over their work, having less authority despite a greater emphasis on local institutional autonomy. Rather than dealing with stress claims, Carr (1993) suggests that the whole notion of educational leadership requires rethinking.

Research respondents presented loud and unanimous calls for governments to eliminate red tape and forms of impersonal accountability that waste time, distract focus, stifle creativity, and frustrate workers' lives. There is also a pervasive skepticism about governmental calls for "productivity" increases which are perceived as code for "working harder and longer" (Heath, 2013; Quiggin, 2011).

Apple (1992, p. 426), focusing on the endpoint of work intensification, aptly captures the paradox:

> Intensification is one of the most tangible ways in which the working conditions of [educators] have eroded. It has many symptoms, from the trivial to the more complex—ranging from having no time at all . . . to a total absence of time to keep up with one's field. We can see it most visibly in the chronic

sense of overload that has escalated over time. This has led to a multitude of results.

Intensification leads people to cut corners so that what is essential to the task *immediately* at hand is accomplished. It forces people to rely on "experts" to tell them what to do and to begin to mistrust the expertise they may have developed over the years. In the process, quality is sacrificed for quantity. Getting done is substituted for work well done.

And as time itself becomes a scarce commodity, isolation grows, thereby reducing the possibility of interaction and discussion among [educators] to jointly share, critique, and rebuild their practices. Often the primary task, to quote one teacher, is to "find a way to get through the day." And, finally, pride itself is jeopardized as the work becomes dominated by someone else's conception of what should be done.

IT'S ABOUT WHAT MATTERS

Time matters as much as money (Goodin et al., 2008). Discretionary time is of the essence—that is, time that is free to spend as individuals please. Bunting (2005, p. 324) calls for individuals being "much more wary of organizations which have developed a fine rhetoric of sloughing off their own responsibilities while at the same time increasing those of their employees." In very many instances, educational institutions and systems fit well into this category. Work that encroaches on personal time (which includes family time) and "put up or shut up" work cultures need to be challenged (Bunting, 2005).

Work intensification is the corporeal manifestation of market economic, neoliberal values—cost efficiency, productivity, value for money, rising consumer expectations, new high-stakes accountabilities and measurement systems, the flexible, adaptable, mobile, nimble, and "lean" education workforce. Education workers are living examples of "the economic dream" and most will toil hard for low pay, compared to other sectors of the workforce.

At the same time, the pervasive infiltration of economic imperatives in education has required institutions to pick up the collateral damage incurred by economic rationalism. Educational institutions play their part in producing an individual's economic and social capital, but they also bear the brunt of the worst excesses of capitalism and respond to meet the needs of their students and communities accordingly.

School breakfast programs, student housing loans, welfare officers and counselors, parenting programs, security guards at the gates, and much, much more are responses stemming from social needs that once were not required or fell outside the realms of education. Educational institutions pick up the pieces and their remit expands accordingly, stretching already tight human resources—time and budgets—even further.

Given the expanding and increasingly essential role that educators play in our communities, it is surprising and disappointing that they so rarely receive the praise and social respect they deserve (even though broad-scale questionnaires consistently reveal that teachers, alongside nurses and pharmacists, are perceived as the most honest and ethical of all professionals.) (Conversely, members of Congress, political lobbyists, and state officials, alongside used-car salespeople, rank as the least honest and ethical); see, for example, Gallup, 2014)).

Working long hours reduces productivity, attendance, and commitment at work AND life expectancy (*The Economist*, 2013c; OECD 2012b). The more agency and control employees have over their work, and the higher the sense of teamwork and camaraderie they experience, the fewer cases of stress reported (Schaufeldi, Maslach & Tadeusz, 1996).

There are many calls for change. Positive schools, positive psychology (focusing on values such as wisdom, courage, humanity, justice, temperance, and transcendence), and the importance of happiness are fast gaining traction in education (see for example, Huebner, Gillman, Reschly & Hall, 2009; Noddings, 2003; Preiss, 2012a; Reivich, Gillham, Chaplin & Seligman, 2005; Van Nieuwerburgh, 2012). But these are remedies that strike at effects, not causes.

What matters most in human lives—family and loving relationships, friends and community, fulfilling employment, a safe and sustainable environment, leisure time, good health, and education for the sake of it—all contribute to well-being and happiness. These are things for which educators have less time, and they are not measured or accounted for, but perhaps they should be.

For example, there is increasing commentary on whether gross domestic product (a metric based on national economic production and consumption or the national "bottom line") as a measure of national "progress" is adequate (Dean, 2014). Going right against the hegemonic trend, however, and striking at the elemental foundations of human lives, Bhutan measures public happiness—"gross national happiness" (GNH) instead of GDP. Public policy initiatives must first pass review via a GNH impact statement (the human-happiness equivalent of an environmental impact statement) before being accepted for implementation.

GNH promotes peace, sustainable development, cultural values, conservation of the natural environment, and good governance. It measures well-being and happiness as they relate to quality of life (see for example, Adler Braun, 2009; Ezechieli, 2003; Zencey, 2009). Imagine how lives would change with collective human happiness as the measure of policy success!

Costanza, Hart, Posner and Talberth (2009) also highlight the flaws in GDP, suggesting it be replaced instead with the Genuine Progress Indicator (GPI), which measures economic activity, including nonpaid economic activities, additions and subtractions based on the sustainability of economic pursuits, and impacts on the well-being of the population and the environment. GPI calibrates national debt in terms of purpose, with investment, such as public infrastructure, being a plus and consumption incurring a minus (see also Costanza et al., 2004).

Importantly for the focus of this book, GPI measures the benefits of education. On this measure, while GDP has been steadily rising, GPI has decreased progressively since the 1970s (Dean, 2014). Dean (2014) argues that the benefits of GDP have benefited sections of the population disproportionately, and that while powerful players may not be keen to abandon GDP for GPI, it would be beneficial for governments to prepare and release both indicators for comparison. His summation:

> As Peter Drucker, one of the 20th century's leading thinkers on business and management, said: "What gets measured gets managed." Measuring what really matters would have knock-on effects on how we manage taxation, education, public investment, the environment and ultimately on how we live our lives, giving us a genuinely richer and more sustainable society, and one in which we have the ability to pursue those things that actually do make life worth living.

Similarly, Robert F. Kennedy sought to address material poverty, but also to "confront the poverty of satisfaction—purpose and dignity—that afflicts us all"—and he questioned "the mere accumulation of material things" (Kennedy, 1968). In the same speech he criticized GDP as a measure of judgment, pointing out the destruction created in its wake, such as environmental degradation, urban sprawl, income inequality, the proliferation of violence, or elisions to important contributions such as child rearing, housework, and community service. It:

> does not allow for the health of our children, the quality of their education or the joy of their play. It does not include the beauty of our poetry or the strength of our marriages, the intelligence of our public debate or the integrity of our public officials. It measures neither our wit nor our courage, neither our wisdom nor our learning, neither our compassion nor our devotion to our country, it measures everything in short, except that which makes life worthwhile. (Kennedy, 1968)

IN CONCLUSION

Goldin (in Kendall, 2013) suggests that the world is at the crossroad. There has never been a more propitious time than this century to improve living standards for the world's population: millions of people getting out of poverty and people living longer through medical availability and capacity, for example.

Concurrently and conversely, in a hyper-globalized world, Goldin argues it is also possible to foresee the worst century ever looming and perhaps even to face complete annihilation: expanding consumption, growth and pollution, climate change, greater disease and antibiotic resistance, financial freedoms, and youth unemployment creating more catastrophic economic crashes than seen in the past, and governmental short-termism and the twenty-four-hour media cycle deflecting and deterring politicians and public decision makers from making sensible, long-term, essential changes.

Respondents from the research projects on which this book is based suggested some very simple things that they believed would make a difference in their working lives:

- more resources (particularly administration support—less "administrivia");
- more realistic work expectations;
- more flexible employment options and work practices that enable an improved work-life balance;
- more professional autonomy and trust at the individual and institutional level;
- greater recognition, respect, and thanks for efforts and achievements;
- better support policies and procedures in regard to replacing absent staff;
- improved professional development, induction, and mentoring opportunities; and
- support and time to work with colleagues in teams.

These suggestions appear to not be asking too much, but would, in the opinion of education workers, make working and personal lives happier, more productive, and more rewarding.

Chapter Ten

The Genie Is Out of the Bottle: Game-Changing Paradox, Dissonance and Dissent

> There is always an easy solution to every human problem—neat, plausible and wrong.
> —H. L. Mencken

This book has described numerous contradictions in education policy aims and practices that produce paradoxical effects. With every goodwill to improve education and educational outcomes, policy contradictions are actually creating confusion and often the opposite outcomes to those planned.

There are policies that encounter endorsement from educational leaders, while others meet their condemnation. Some policies aid education and add to the satisfaction of educators, while others add confusion and make the work of educators more difficult. Education policies paradoxically undermine each other. For educational institutions, educational leaders and governors, teachers and academics, the end game is tail spinning as policy reforms and endless restructurings demand major change on top of the quotidian teaching, learning, student support, and administration.

Overcommitted, intensified work conditions, rising expectations, and the increasingly difficult task of focusing on "core business" are having deleterious, game-changing effects.

Drivers of change have emerged and grown on the tide of globalization. These include:

- increasing competition among traditional educational institutions and new private market players;

- challenges and competition for traditional sources of funding;
- disruptive technological capabilities providing ubiquitous access to, production of, support for, and dissemination of, knowledge;
- the global mobility of students and education employees;
- the rapidly diversified and expanding participation rates of students of increasing ages;
- new players at different phases of the education value chain—content production, teaching/content dissemination, certification, etc.;
- the commercialization of education brands, trademarks, products, programs, and research;
- expectations of contextualized, individualized student choices and experiences; and
- a fast growing, mobile world population amidst concerns about the sustainability of the planet.

Resultant rapid changes have disrupted traditional power bases and long held hegemonic assumptions and understandings about education. More than this, perhaps some important characteristics of education have been lost or are struggling to remain viable—aspects of education such as a comprehensive curriculum, respect for authentic learning, inquiry and pedagogy, education equity, and sound investment in education and ancillary support services.

Irreversible transformation is very threatening, and it is human nature to resist change. Beare (2010) argues that the natural human instinct is to try to simplify things so they are understandable and to revert to tried and true, safe strategies. In times of great flux, it is common to see governments, the media, and the public crying out for a return to past conservative choices. It is reassuring to return to what is known and has been known.

The problem, as Beare suggests, is that the past will never come again. The moment is only provisional—we are continually rethinking and reshaping the world. The world keeps changing and, subsequently, individuals are transformed and are always adjusting. Lives are in a constant process of finding and negotiating politics; with directions forward always being clouded because they are beyond the borders of our once clear knowledge and understanding.

Thus, Eisenstein (2010) argues that a politics of audaciousness—audacious thinking and action—is required. Audaciousness concedes the constancy of major change in the world: the new, the innovative, the re-scoped, the uncharted, the stuff that makes us stop and think, that unsettles us and makes us look more closely. In such audacious times, locations and structures of power change to be occupied by different people in new ways.

We become filled with doubt as our questions cannot be answered accurately. But possibilities created during such times are unlocked as individuals adapt and structural constraints mutate. Possibilities are opened up because former constructions are undermined and challenged in unconventional ways, hence loosening their clarity and certainty. The politics will be different but never fully resolved. Things will always be messy and complicated—there are restrictions and breakouts, and some events will continue to be unplanned and unexpected.

But Eisenstein's advice is to be aware of the importance of doubt. When we doubt that we understand, when we have to think and are unsettled, social change is inevitable. This research suggests that for those who lead, manage, and govern education, such a time has arrived. A constant critical consideration will be the interests that our actions are serving.

Educational leaders, business managers, and governors must make it their business to keep key decision makers accurately informed through local, national, and international means and by using collective evidence to make strong claims for "disruptive" and "audacious" policy determinations.

Education, health, employment, and the environment will be the most pressing areas for long-term change and innovative action. As it stands now, education is too much a victim of "short-termism." Untested ideas or hunches are launched for implementation in or on educational institutions with too little time to ever be fully enacted or proven to work or not before they are overturned for new ones (Albury in Kendall, 2013).

At this juncture, several interrelated thoughts come to mind as the contents of this book are summed up. There exists a pervasive sense of *desuetude* among the educational leaders interviewed—a strong sense that something important is being evaded—that essentially significant features of education are being neglected or abandoned.

At the heart of this feeling is the inimicality of market values and education practice, with the needs of the latter involving taking responsibility for individuals, communities, collective stewardship, and safekeeping. This concerns "the commons"—the cultural, social, and environmental aspects of life that are shared; a view that places community, people, the environment, and other living things as the most important aspects of life and which should form the basis of public policy.

Much of this sentiment is lost in current education policy. There's a feeling that the fox is in the henhouse—that education policy has lost perspective on what is valuable and important and is losing its way.

Another thought concerns the Faustian dilemma (based on the Faustian choice of trading one's soul with the Devil in exchange for wealth and power). Education policy has (unwittingly perhaps) traded something very precious for something that is not so valuable. The Faustian dilemma serves as an analogy for the current education policy dilemma. Has the baby been thrown out with the bathwater? Have we jumped from the frying pan into the fire?

There is also a sense that "open" systems that operated in education have been replaced by "closed" systems (see Postman & Weingartner, 1969). Those leading and managing educational institutions have influence onsite, but believe they exert too little influence in systemic policy determinations. Determinism, rationality, objectivity, and certainty have trumped creativity, subjectivity, and the professional judgment of educators. "Consultation" (at best) and receiving mandated instructions (at worst) is not as professionally rewarding or respectful as collaboration and cooperation at all levels of education.

Much is at stake if educators cannot be fully engaged with all education processes, especially concerning policies for which they are responsible and that shape institutional life and learning. Recent emphases on risk management are a clear example of the closed system hegemony that creates further risk as it aims to eradicate and reduce it—a further paradox (see Starr, 2012a). Openness needs to be reasserted; debate and risk taking encouraged.

The processes of policy formation are mistrusted. Throughout interview transcripts, there is an overwhelming sense of untenable distrust in governments at all levels and of all persuasions in doing what is best in education for the populations they serve. There are generally two ends of the values spectrum represented in each of the policy paradoxes in this book, and educators are clearly, and perhaps not unsurprisingly, more inclined toward those supporting social ends and the common weal.

This is not a blinkered leftist response—interviewees were as critical of so-called progressive left-leaning governments as they were of conservative governments. The reason behind this is that education policies from either side of the political spectrum are surprisingly similar and stem from the same neoliberal, free-market bases. Distrust derives from the fact that education policy emanates from the whim of politicians, their sense of populist concerns, and the predictable recommendations of their hand-chosen consultants, rather than from actual needs, the view of practitioners, or independent academic researchers, who are marginalized.

Change is most successful when it involves those charged with enacting it. In this case, the 'implementers" are not involved in policy formation, in analyzing the information on which determinations are based, or in the direction inherent in education policy practices. Distributed leadership should be taken to its logical conclusion such that education policy making is not a centralized, closed process, but one that valorizes the voices and involvement of practitioners.

Misguided perceptions often become the basis for policy development and revisions, and their effects can be damaging. Furthermore, commentators such as Evans and Giroux (2013) argue that the literatures of academic researchers and the population at large rarely come together, and that in order to create change and encourage social debate, there should be more crossover between the two.

Policy aims should be extracted from the sole preserve of government appointed policy "experts" who do not work in educational institutions. And policy debates should be based on proper evidence—an authentic research base that recognizes the praxis of educators, engaged scholarship, and professional reflection as valid "evidence." Clearly, there is a marked mismatch of education visions on a grand scale. The policy paradoxes created represent an immaculate vicious circle.

Sir Ken Robinson (2010) argues that people learn and work best when learning and work speaks to their authentic self and when it is something to be enjoyed and not endured. But he says, "We have sold ourselves into a fast model of education, and it's impoverishing our spirits and our energy as much as fast food is depleting our physical bodies."

Decades of education research are deliberately sidelined when conclusive evidence disrupts current policy trajectories. Research respondents believe we are witnessing a deliberate strategy to further marketize education. Education policy will aid the economic, ideological, and financial ambitions of governments. In the process, education is being changed irrevocably. As Dinham (2014, pp. 1–2) argues:

> If these developments continue then the inevitable outcomes will be greater inequity and continuing decline in educational performance, something that will provide the proponents for such change with further "evidence" to support their position and for even more far-reaching change. . . .
>
> A tsunami comprises waves with very long wave lengths. Often these go unnoticed until it is too late to do anything about them. When they reach land great devastation can result. The "long wave" changes to education . . . need to be subjected to intense scrutiny before it is too late. If the profession remains silent and passive in the face of some of these developments we will only have ourselves to blame for what might eventuate.

"Bad" education policy should be challenged and addressed rather than tolerated, but educators have been slow in publicly defining programs that work and what does not. Rarely do educators have, or take the opportunity to, dispel or discredit inaccurate reporting or opinion with accurate information and professional knowledge from the field.

This is a great pity, and the cause probably comes down to being simply too busy. And there are no two-way feedback loops—no upward accountability. Politicians and governments come and go, but policies can meanwhile create mayhem without consequence for their originators.

The game-changers are too significant to be waylaid by electoral politics. Needed are governments that are fit for purpose, with accountability and transparency being a two-way street, with policy makers held to the greatest levels of accountability for their impactful decisions. The blinkered, cognitive dissonance witnessed currently cannot go on without consequence. New accountabilities for policy outcomes need to be built into political decisions. However, there are also calls for education to be independent from political party agendas and removed from the political arena altogether (see for example, Kendall, 2013).

There is a need to build a different kind of evidence base derived from practitioners to prove new points, without sole resort to decontextualized tests and audits (Mitchell, 2013). There is a need to be more active and more critical in public, overt ways to reestablish proper agency in education policy pursuits. This will be a collective effort and one that operates in concert, while being respectful and appreciative of differences and diversity. There is also a case for turning pervasive generalized beliefs and macro statistics to the advantage of educational institutions, rather than having them held up for more criticism.

Respondents in this research call for broad discussion and debate beyond the political class about the purposes of education. What is education for? And who is education for? The values and ideology underpinning education policy are being called into question—should the foundational values of education concern the social and cultural aspects of life, or should they be founded on market and neoliberal premises (see Reid, 2005)?

Education represents and embodies everyone's interests, so there is a case for policy contradiction, paradox, and ill-informed assumptions to be exposed and highlighted. Hence, it is imperative to educate adults—the parents, students, politicians, the Fourth Estate, the "commentariat," and other stakeholders—about what really matters in education, what should be done, what should not be done, with supporting self-generated evidence and data from local contexts.

While the immediate education context is the prime focus of educators, there is also a need to extend the purview beyond the institutional gate, beyond that of the local community, the state, or the nation. Educational leaders and business managers, their professional associations, and the communities they serve have a role in advocating on behalf of education and educators, and for learning in its broadest sense, for all children and students everywhere.

It is a sad indictment that the world still is nowhere near reaching the UNESCO millennium goal of attaining primary school education for all the world's children by 2015. It is estimated that fifty-seven million children have no access to education. This is a disgrace and will be further frustrated by rapid world population growth. Addressing this policy dilemma must be high on the urgent global educational to do list. It makes sense that the most resources should go to the sites most in need, otherwise the dire negative effects of disenfranchisement will persist.

Current education and other social policies steeped in competition and individualism are selfish dogmas that foster a clamoring for advantage in the social psyche. To break the gridlock requires more altruism, a greater concern for the world's people and a recalibration of economic impacts on environments, communities, and long-term sustainability. Education at all levels has an enormous role to play in any future, but some urgent policy responses are required.

This research detected undeniable undercurrents of disappointment and frustration among education practitioners. Education should not be a drag. It is about the joy of living—the wonder and excitement of life and being alive. Education is most effective when it is enjoyable, applicable, relevant, and interesting (see Postman, 1995). It should be concerned about happiness.

Education game-changers present opportunities to travel paths other than those being followed, but the policy aims they inspire currently are narrow and misdirected. As Noddings (2003, p. 84) aptly argues: "There is more to individual life and the life of the nation then economic superiority."

References

33rd Square (2013). *Alvin Toffler on accelerating change*. 18 April, 2013, 33rdsquare.com Retrieved on 25 August, 2013 from http://www.33rdsquare.com/2013/04/alvin-toffler-on-accelerating-change.html.

Adams, R. (2013). Disadvantaged schools face uphill struggle to meet GCSE targets. *The Guardian*, 24 August, 2013.

Adler Braun, A. (2009). Gross National Happiness in Bhutan: A living example of an alternative approach to progress, 24 September, 2009. Retrieved on 26 February, 2014 from http://www.grossnationalhappiness.com/OtherArticles/GNHPaperbyAlejandro.pdf.

Anderson, J. & Rainie, L. (2012). *Millennials will benefit and suffer due to their hyperconnected lives*. Pew Research Center, Washington, DC: Pew Internet and American Life Project.

Anderson, J. C. (2010). *The de-cluttered school: How to create a cleaner, calmer and greener learning environment*. London: Continuum International Publishing Group.

Angwin, J. (2010). The web's new gold mine: your secrets. *Washington Post*, 30 July, 2010.

Aoun, J. E. (2013). A shakeup of higher education. *Boston Globe*, 17 November, 2013.

Apple, M. W. (1992). Do the standards go far enough? Power, policy, and practice in mathematics education. *Journal for Research in Mathematics Education*, 23(5), 412–31.

———. (2004) *Ideology and Curriculum*, 3rd edition. New York: Routledge Falmer.

Argyris, C. (1998). Empowerment: The emperor's new clothes. *Harvard Business Review*, May–June 1998, 98–105.

Asbury, K., Gladwell, M. & Goldin, I. (2013). Advantage. *The Forum*, BBC World Service, 11 November, 2013. Retrieved on 12 November, 2013 from http://www.bbc.co.uk/programmes/p01ksh9h.

Australian Broadcasting Corporation (ABC) (2011). The interview. *Sunday Nights with John Cleary*, ABC 774, Melbourne, 14 August, 2011.

Australian Broadcasting Corporation (ABC) (2013a). Free training as secondary teachers shortage looms. Australian Broadcasting Corporation, 7 June, 2013. Retrieved on 7 June, 2013 from http://www.abc.net.au/news/2013-06-07/shortage-of-high-school-teachers-prompts-free-training/4740190?section=wa.

Australian Broadcasting Corporation (ABC) (2013b). Parties reject call to close small schools to fund literacy specialists. Australian Broadcasting Corporation, 23 September 2013. Retrieved on 23 September, 2013 from http://www.abc.net.au/news/2013-09-22/revelations-half-of-tasmanians-are-illiterate/4973600.

Australian Broadcasting Corporation (ABC) (2013c). Universities to woo more international students. Australian Broadcasting Corporation, *News*, 7 June, 2013. Retrieved on 6 Decem-

ber, 2013 from http://www.abc.net.au/news/2013-06-07/universities-to-woo-more-international-students/4740718?section=act.
Australian Curriculum, Assessment and Reporting Authority (ACARA) (2012). *Report of 2012 NAPLAN Test incidents*. Retrieved on 5 October, 2013 from http://www.acara.edu.au/verve/_resources/2012_NAPLAN_TEST_INCIDENTS_REPORT_website_version.pdf.
Australian Government (2012). *Australia in the Asian century*. Canberra, ACT: Department of Prime Minister and Cabinet, Australian Government, October 2012.
Baier, A. (1994). *Moral prejudices: Essays on ethics*. Cambridge, MA: Harvard University Press.
Balfour, C. (2012). Acacia College compo claim fears. *Whittlesea Leader*, 26 October, 2012, p. 1.
Ball, S. J. (1987). *The micro-politics of the school: Towards a theory of school organization*. London: Routledge.
Ball, S. (1993). Education markets, choice and social class: The market as a class strategy in the UK and the USA. *British Journal of Sociology of Education*, 14(1), 3–19.
———. (1994). *Education reform: A critical and post-structural approach*. Buckingham, UK: Open University Press.
———. (2010). *Education policy and social class: The selected works of Stephen J. Ball*. Abingdon, UK: Routledge.
Bastian, D. (2014). Ranking reveal—from the top 3. *Campus Review*, 24 February, 2014.
Bauerlein, V. (2013). College properties up for sale. *Wall Street Journal*, 1 November, 2013, A3.
Beare, H. (2010). *Six decades of continuous restructuring: Swimming through waves of reform without being drowned*. Australian Council for Educational Leaders Monograph series, No. 46. Penrith, BC, NSW: Australian Council for Educational Leaders.
Belfield, C. R. & Levin, H. L. (2002). *Education privatization: Causes, consequences and planning implications*. Paris: UNESCO.
Bentham, J. (1995). Panoptican. In Bozovic, M. (Ed.). *The Panoptican Writings*. London: Verso, 29–95.
Berg, J. (2013). Crowd source peer-to-peer assessment in MOOCs? *Scholar*, 27 August, 2013. Retrieved 27 August 2013 from https://cgscholar.com/community/cg_community/profiles/jason-berg/updates/5752.
Birchenough, C. (1914). *History of elementary education in England and Wales from 1800 to the present day*. London: W. B. Clive.
Bligh, D. A. (1998). *What's the use of lectures?* 5th Edition. Exeter, UK: Intellect.
Bohle, S. (2013). Librarians and the era of the MOOC. Scilogs. Retrieved on 23 August 2013 from http://www.scilogs.com/scientific_and_medical_libraries/librarians-and-the-era-of-the-mooc/.
Bohn, S., Reyes, B. & Johnson, H. (2013). *The impact of budget cuts on California's community colleges*. Los Angeles: Public Policy Institute of California.
Bokor, J. (2012). *University of the future: A thousand year old industry on the cusp of profound change*. Melbourne, Victoria: Ernst & Young.
Bonnor, C. (2013). Misguided schools "market" sees us slip down the ranks. *Sydney Morning Herald*, 9 December, 2013.
Botsman, R. & Rogers, R. (2010). *What's mine is yours: The rise of collaborative consumption*. Hammersmith, UK: HarperCollins.
Bottery, M. (1994). *Lessons for schools? A comparison of business and educational management*. London: Cassell.
———. (2011). Refocusing educational leadership in an age of overshoot: Embracing an education for sustainable development. *International Studies in Educational Administration*, 39(2), 3–6.
———. (2012). Leadership, the logic of sufficiency and the sustainability of education. *Educational Management, Administration & Leadership*, 40(4), 449–63.
Bowen, W. G., Kurzweil, M. A. & Tobin, E. M. (2005). *Equity and excellence in American higher education*. Charlottesville, Virginia: University of Virginia Press.

References

Bower, J. & Christensen, C. M. (1995). Disruptive technologies: Catching the wave. *Harvard Business Review*, January 1995.

Bowles, S. & Gintis, H. (1976). *Schooling in Capitalist America: educational reform and the contradictions of economic life*. New York: Basic Books.

Brill, S. (2010). The teachers' unions' last stand. *New York Times*, 17 May, 2010.

Brown, K., Benkovitz, J., Muttillo, A. J. & Urban, T. (2011). Leading schools of excellence and equity: Documenting effective strategies in closing achievement gaps. *Teachers College Record*, 113(1), January 2011, 57–96.

Brown, M., Ralph, S. & Brember, I. (2002). Change-linked work-related stress in British teachers. *Research in Education*, University of Manchester, 67, May 2002, 1–12.

Brynjolfsson, E. (1993). The productivity paradox of information technology. *Communications of the ACM*, 36(12), 66–77.

Buckingham, J. (2014a). *Target 30: Reducing the burden for future generations: School funding on a budget*. St. Leonards, NSW: The Centre for Independent Studies.

———. (2014b). Why can't wealthy parents pay for public schooling? *The Drum*, 5 May, 2014. Retrieved on 5 May, 2014 from http://www.abc.net.au/news/2014-05-05/buckingham-why-cant-wealthy-parents-pay-for-public-schooling/5430484.

Bullock, A. D. & Thomas, H. (1997). Evaluating Educational Reforms. In *Educational Reforms in England and Wales: A briefing with commentary*. Department for International Development Report, DFID: London, UK, 54–59.

Bunting, M. (2005). *Willing slaves: How the overwork culture is ruling our lives*. Hammersmith, UK: HarperPerennial.

Burke, R. J. & Cooper, C. L. (Eds). (2008). *The long work hours culture: Causes, consequences and choices*. Bingley, UK: Emerald Group Publishing.

Bush, T. (2008). From management to leadership: Semantic or meaningful change? *Educational Management, Administration and Leadership*, 36(2), 271–88.

Bushnell, M. (2003). Teachers in the schoolhouse Panopticon: Complicity and resistance. *Education and Urban Society*, 35(3), 251–72.

Butler, E. (1983). *Hayek: His contribution to the political and economic thought of our time*. London: Temple Smith.

Cabanac, G. & Hartley, J. (2013). Issues of work-life balance among JASIST authors and editors. *Journal of the American Society for Information Science and Technology*, 64(10), 2182–86.

Cadwalladr, C. (2012). Do online courses spell the end of the traditional university? *The Observer*, 11 November, 2012.

Caldwell, B. (2011). Private schools and the future of public education in Australia. *Phi Delta Kappan*, May 2011, 92(8), 95–96.

———. (2013a). Let's bring on a real education revolution. *The Age*, 16 August, 2013.

———. (2013b). *Leadership and governance in the self-transforming school*. Presentation to the Australian Council of Educational Leaders, Canberra, ACT, 4 October, 2013.

Caldwell, B. & Spinks, J. (1986). *Policy formation and resource allocation*. Geelong, Victoria: Deakin University Press.

———. (1988). *The self-managing school*. Lewes, UK: Falmer Press.

Campbell, C. Proctor, H. & Sherington, G. (2009). *School choice: How parents negotiate the new school market in Australia*. Crows Nest, NSW: Allen & Unwin.

Career NZ (2013). *Skills employers are looking for*. Retrieved on 5 December, 2013 from http://www.careers.govt.nz/plan-your-career/not-sure-what-to-do/skills-employers-are-looking-for/.

Carlson, C. (2014). Five Hammond principals to lose posts. *Post Tribune*, 24 January, 2014.

Carr, A. (1993). Stress and the school principal. *Principal Matters*, 5(3), December 1993.

Carr, S. (2010). *Personalisation, productivity and efficiency*. London: Social Care Institute for Excellence.

Chilcott, T. (2013). State school mental anguish costs $2m in workers compensation payouts. *The Courier Mail*, 16 July, 2013.

———. (2014a). Move to restrict school rankings. *Courier Mail*, 28 March, 2014, p. 15.

References

———. (2014b). Schools focus on three Rs and rote learning under NAPLAN test regime. *Courier Mail*, 12 May, 2014.
Chomsky, N. (1992). *How the world works*. Brooklyn, NY: Soft Skull Press.
Chua, A. (2011). *Battle hymn of the Tiger Mother*. New York: Penguin.
Conklin, J. (2005). *Dialogue mapping: building shared understanding of wicked problems*, 1st edition. New York: Wiley.
Connell, R. W. (1998). Schools, markets, justice: Education in a fractured world. In Reid, A. (Ed.). *Going public: Education policy and public education in Australia*. Deakin West, ACT: ACSA.
Connell, R. W., Ashenden, D. J., Kessler, S. & Dowsett, G. W. (1982). *Making the difference: Schools, families and social division*. North Sydney, NSW: Allen & Unwin.
Cooperative Education Service Agency (CESA) (2010). *Transforming Public Education: A Regional Call to Action*. Luxemburg, WI: CESA.
Corbin, J. & Strauss, A. (2008). *Basics of qualitative research*, 3rd edition. Sage: Thousand Oaks, CA.
Costanza, R., Hart, M., Posner, S. & Talberth, J. (2009). *Beyond GDP: The need for new measures of progress*. The Pardee Papers, No. 4, January 2009. Boston: The Frederick S. Pardee Center for the Study of Longer-range Future, Boston University.
Costanza, R., Erickson, J., Fligger, K., Adams, A., Adams, C., Altschuler, B., Balter, S., Fisher, B., Hike, J., Kelly, J., Kerr, T., McCauley, M., Montone, K., Rauch, M., Schmiedeskamp, K., Saxton, D., Sparacino, L., Tusinski, W. & Williams, L. (2004). Estimates of the Genuine Progress Indicator (GPI) for Vermont, Chittenden County and Burlington, from 1950 to 2000. *Ecological Economics*, 51 (2004), 139–55.
Coulson, A. (2011). *The impact of federal involvement in America's classrooms*. Washington, DC: CATO Institute.
Craven, G. (2014). "Teacher education review" high-stakes Q&A. *Campus Review*, 28 April, 2014.
Creed, M. (2013). Streamlining the business of education. *Technology Spectator*, 20 June, 2013. Retrieved on 23 September, 2013 from http://www.businessspectator.com.au/article/2013/6/20/technology/streamlining-business-education.
Crutzen, P. J. (2006). Albedo enhancement by stratospheric sulfur injections: A contribution to resolve a policy dilemma. *Climate Change*, 77(3–4), August 2006, 211–20.
Cutter-MacKenzie, A. (2010a). Australian waste wise schools program: Its past, present, and future. *The Journal of Environmental Education*, 41(3), 165–78.
———. (2010b). Teaching for environmental sustainability. In Gilbert, R. & Hoepper, B. (Eds.). *Teaching Society and Environment*, 4th Edition. South Melbourne, Victoria: Cengage, 348–63.
Dane, J. (2013). Stop worrying and love the MOOC. *Campus Review*, 27 August, 2013.
Darling-Hammond, L. (2006). *Powerful teacher education: Lessons from exemplary programs*. San Francisco: Wiley.
Davie, L. (2013). Why the next big thing in computing is conversation. Fast Company. Retrieved on 5 September, 2013 from http://www.fastcolabs.com/3016702/why-the-next-big-thing-in-computing-is-conversation?partner=newsletter.
Dean, T. (2014). Dethroning GDP as our measure of progress. *The Drum*, 16 January, 2014. Retrieved on 21 January, 2014 from http://www.abc.net.au/news/2014-01-16/dean-dethroning-gdp-as-our-measure-of-progress/5201564.
Department of Education (DoE) (2010). *The importance of teaching: The schools white paper 2010*. London, UK: Department of Education.
Department of Education and Early Childhood Development (DEECD). (2012). New directions for school leadership and the teaching profession. Discussion paper, June 2012. DEECD, Victoria: State of Victoria.
Department of Education and Training (DET) (2004). *The Privilege and the Price*. Melbourne, Victoria: Department of Education and Training, Victoria.
Department of Education, Employment and Workplace Relations (DEEWR) (2010). Higher Education Policy. Retrieved on 17 December, 2010 from http://www.deewr.gov.au/HigherEducation/Policy/Documents/.

Department of Employment, Education and Training (DEET) (1990). *A fair chance for all*. Canberra, ACT: DEET.
DeSaxe, D. (2013). US Head Start program hit with sequester cuts. World Socialist Web Site, 16 April, 2013. Retrieved on 10 April, 2014 from https://www.wsws.org/en/articles/2013/04/16/hsta-a16.html.
Dill, D. D. (2009). Convergence and diversity: The role and influence of university rankings. In Kehm, B. M. & Stensaker, B. (Eds.). (2009). *University rankings, diversity, and the new landscape of higher education*. Rotterdam: Sense Publishers.
Dillon, N. (2008). Hard times, hard cuts uncharted territory. *American School Board Journal*. 195(5), 28–32.
Dinham, S. (2014). Why free market will not fix problems with teachers and teaching. *The Age*, 2 April, 2014.
Dodd, T. (2014). Women locked in low-paid jobs. *Financial Review*, 24 February, 2014.
Druschel, P., Backes, M. & Tirtea, R. (2012). *The right to be forgotten — between expectations and practice*. Crete, Greece: European Network and Information Security Agency.
Duan, P. (2013). What's causing social segregation in our schools? *Online Opinion*, 17 June, 2013. Retrieved on 21 January, 2014 from http://www.onlineopinion.com.au/view.asp?article=15132.
Eggers, D. & Clements Calegari, N. (2011). The high cost of low teacher salaries. *New York Times*, 30 April, 2011.
Eisenstein, Z. (2010). Audacious Feminisms: And their newest sexes, races, genders and globes. Keynote address presented at the Australian Women's and Gender Studies Conference, Hawke Centre, University of South Australia, North Terrace, Adelaide, 29 June–2 July, 2010.
Emerson, D. (2013). Cuts to GST share hit health, education. *West Australian*, 3 July, 2013.
Engelhardt, N. L. & Engelhardt, N. L. Jr. (1940). *Planning the community school*. New York: American Book Company.
Evans, B. & Giroux, H. (2013). Brad Evans and Henry Giroux conversation, 16 January, 2013. Retrieved 10 April 2014 from http://www.youtube.com/watch?v=qoqMbO-2J48.
Ezechieli, E. (2003). *Beyond sustainable development: Education for Gross National Happiness in Bhutan*. Stanford, CA: Stanford University.
Fear, J. & Denniss, R. (2009). *Something for nothing—unpaid overtime in Australia*, Policy Brief No. 7, November 2009. The Australia Institute.
Ferrari, J. (2013). Expert public school teachers to earn $100,000. *The Australian*, 4 December, 2013, p. 5.
Firth, V. & Huntley, R. (2014). *Who's afraid of the public school? Public perceptions of education in Australia*. Surry Hills, NSW: Per Capita.
Fitzgerald, T. (2012). Continuing challenges. In Fitzgerald, T., White, J. & Gunter, H. M. (2012). *Hard labour? Academic work and the changing landscape of higher education*. Bingley, UK: Emerald Group Publishing.
Fitzgerald, T., White, J. & Gunter, H. M. (2012). *Hard labour? Academic work and the changing landscape of higher education*. Bingley, UK: Emerald Group Publishing.
Franzway, S. (2001). *Sexual politics and greedy institutions*. Sydney, NSW: Pluto Press.
Franzway, S., Court, D. & Connell, R. W. (1989). *Staking a claim: Feminism, bureaucracy and the state*. Boston: Allen & Unwin.
Fraser, N. (1989). *Unruly practices: Power, discourse and gender in contemporary social theory*. Cambridge: Polity Press.
Fray, P. (2014). Fiscal crisis? It really depends who you talk to. *The Australian, Oz Fact Checker*, 2 May, 2014, 1–2.
Freeman, R. (2008). *Labour productivity indicators*. Paris: OECD.
Friedman, T. L. (2013). Revolution hits the universities: MOOCs. *The Daily Riff*, 28 January, 2013. Retrieved on 29 August, 2013 from http://www.thedailyriff.com/articles/revolution-hits-the-universities-tom-friedman-declares-1010.php.
Gallup (2014). Honesty/ethics in professions: Gallup historical trends. 17 April, 2014. Retrieved on 18 April, 2014 from http://www.gallup.com/poll/1654/honesty-ethics-professions.aspx.

Gard, M. (2013). Non-core demands overload teachers. *Sydney Morning Herald*, 3 June, 2013.
Gates, B. (2011a). Educational economics: Where do school funds go? Gatesnotes: The blog of Bill Gates, 1 March, 2011. Retrieved on 5 March, 2014 from http://www.gatesnotes.com/Books/Where-Do-School-Funds-Go-Book-Review.
———. (2011b). The wicked problem of school funding. Gatesnotes: The blog of Bill Gates, 1 March, 2011. Retrieved on 5 March, 2014 from http://www.gatesnotes.com/Education/Marguerite-Roza-Education-Funding-Wicked-Problem.
Gillespie, D. (2014). *Free schools: How to get a great education for your kids without spending a fortune*. Sydney, NSW: Macmillan.
Giroux, H. A. (1981). *Ideology, Culture, and the Process of Schooling*. Philadelphia: Temple University Press.
———. (2013a). When schools become dead zones of the imagination: A critical pedagogy manifesto. Truthout, 13 August, 2013. Retrieved on 10 April, 2014 from http://www.truth-out.org/opinion/item/18133-when-schools-become-dead-zones-of-the-imagination-a-critical-pedagogy-manifesto.
———. (2013b). *America's education deficit and the war on youth: Beyond electoral politics*. New York: Monthly Review Press.
Glaser, B. & Strauss, A. (1967). *The discovery of grounded theory*. Chicago: Aldine
Glatter, R. (2006). Leadership and organization in education: Time for re-orientation? *School Leadership & Management*, 26(1), 69–83.
Gombrich, C. (2012). Interdisciplinarity and individuation. 16 January, 2012, *Carl Gombrich: Education, Interdisciplinarity, Expertise*. Retrieved 5 February, 2013 from http://www.carlgombrich.org/interdisciplinarity-and-individuation/.
Goodin, R. E., Rice, J. M., Parpo, A. & Eriksson, L. (2008). *Discretionary time: A new measure of freedom*. Cambridge, UK: Cambridge Press.
Grande, P. (2014). *Phil's Gang Radio Show*, 6 January, 2014, Radio KGU, Honolulu, Hawaii.
Grattan, M., Tomazin, F. & Harrison, D. (2008). School v school: PM's rule. *The Age*, 28 August, 2008, 1.
Gray, D. E. (2009). *Doing research in the real world*, 2nd edition. London: Sage.
Green, F. (2008). Work effort and worker well-being in the age of affluence. In Burke, R. J. & Cooper, C. L. (Eds). (2008). *The long work hours culture: Causes, consequences and choices*. Bingley, UK: Emerald Group Publishing, 115–36.
Green, R., Toner, P. & Agarwal, R. (2012). *Understanding productivity: Australia's choice*. Sydney, NSW: The McKell Institute, University of Technology, Sydney.
Grimmett, P. P. & D'Amico, L. (2008). Do British Columbia's recent education policy changes enhance professionalism among teachers? *Canadian Journal of Educational Administration and Policy*, Issue 78, July 17, 2008.
Gronn, P. & Lacey, K. (2004). Positioning oneself for leadership: Feelings of vulnerability among aspirant principals. *School Leadership and Management*, 24(4), 405–24.
Groves, N. (2012). Online learning: pedagogy, technology and opening up higher education. *The Guardian, Higher Education Network*, 22 November, 2012.
Grundy, S. (1987). *Curriculum: Product or praxis?* New York: Routledge.
Gunter, H. (2012). Academic work and performance. In Fitzgerald, T., White, J. & Gunter, H. M. (2012). *Hard labour? Academic work and the changing landscape of higher education*. Bingley, UK: Emerald Group Publishing.
Habermas, J. (1987). *Knowledge and human interests*. Trans. J. J. Shapiro. Cambridge: Polity Press.
Hallinger, P. & Snidvongs, K. (2008). Educating leaders: Is there anything to learn from business management? *Educational Management Administration & Leadership*, January 2008, 36, 9–31.
Hamilton, C. (2010). *Requiem for a species: Why we resist the truth about climate change*. Abingdon, UK: Earthscan.
Harrison, D. (2012). A class above. *Sydney Morning Herald*, 17 February, 2013.
Hartley, J. (2013). Are academics working harder than they did before? Or just differently? The Impact Blog, London School of Economics and Political Science. Retrieved on 5 January,

2014 from http://blogs.lse.ac.uk/impactofsocialsciences/2013/12/06/are-academics-working-harder/.
Hayek, F. A. von (1949). *Individualism and the economic order.* London: Routledge & Kegan Paul.
———. (1960). *Prices and Production.* London: Routledge & Kegan Paul.
———. (1979a). *A conversation with Friedrich A. von Hayek: Science and socialism.* Washington, DC: American Enterprise Institute for Public Policy Research.
———. (1979b). *Social justice, socialism and democracy: Three Australian lectures.* Turramurra, NSW: Centre for Independent Studies.
Hayes, D., Mills, M., Christie, P. & Lingard, B. (2006). *Teachers and schooling: making a difference.* Crows Nest, NSW: Allen and Unwin.
Hearn, J. & Parkin, W. (2007). The emotionality of organization violations: Gender relations in practice. In Lewis, P. & Simpson, R. (Eds.). *Gendering emotions in organizations.* Basingstoke, UK: Palgrave Macmillan.
Heath, J. (2013). Pension age may need to rise: Productivity Commission. *Financial Review*, 22 November, 2013, 1.
Henderson, M. (2014). Book review: Assessing the educational data movement. *Teachers College Record*, 24 January, 2014.
Hesse, M. (2010). Keeping up with social networking sites: How much is enough? *Washington Post*, 19 October, 2010.
Hiatt, B. (2013). WA: Parents give millions to a few state schools. *West Australian*, 16 March, 2013.
Hil, R. (2012). *Whackademia: An insider's account of the troubled university.* Sydney, NSW: NewSouth Publishing, University of New South Wales Press.
Hoffman, M. F. & Ford, D. J. (2010). *Organizational rhetoric: Situations and strategies.* Thousand Oaks, CA: Sage.
Hogan, D. & Donovan, C. (2005). The social outcomes of schooling: Subjective agency among Tasmanian adolescents. *Leading and Managing*, 11(2), 84–102.
Hopkins, D., Reynolds, D. & Gray, J. (2005) *School Improvement: Lessons from Research.* London: DfES.
Horn, R. E. (2001). Knowledge mapping for complex social messes, A presentation to the Foundations in the Knowledge Economy conference at the David and Lucile Packard Foundation, 16 July, 2001. Retrieved 2 January, 2012 from http://www.stanford.edu/-rhorn/SpchPackard.html.
Houghton, J. & Gruen, N. (2012). *Transparency and productivity: The effects of open and transparent Public Sector information management practices on costs and productivity.* Carlton South, Victoria: Australia and New Zealand School of Government. Retrieved on 17 December, 2013 from http://www.anzsog.edu.au/media/upload/publication/94_2-Houghton-and-Gruen-Transparency-and-Productivity.pdf.
Huebner, S., Gilman, R., Reschly, A. J. & Hall, R. W. (2009). Positive schools. In Lopez, S. J. & Snyder, C. R. (Eds.) *Oxford handbook of positive psychology,* 2nd edition, 651–58. Oxford, England: Oxford University Press.
Hurst, D. (2013). Back to basics. *The Age*, 28 September, 2013.
Hutton, W. (1995). *The State we're in.* London: Jonathan Cape.
Institute for Policy Studies (2013). *What is public policy? The definition of public policy.* Institute for Policy Studies, Johns Hopkins University, Baltimore, MD. Retrieved 10 April, 2014 from http://ips.jhu.edu/pub/public-policy.
Italie, L. (2008). F-bomb, sexting among new words in *Merriam-Webster Dictionary. The Huffington Post*, 13 August, 2008.
Jobbins, D. (2013). Students shun part-time study as costs soar. *University World News*, 21 March, 2013. Retrieved on 1 April 2014 from http://www.universityworldnews.com/article.php?story=20130320203703651.
Kamenetz, A. (2013). Course choice: The death of public education? Digital/Edu, The Hechinger Report, 1 August, 2013. Retrieved on 1 August, 2013 from http://digital.hechingerreport.org/content/course-choice-the-death-knell-of-public-education_789/?utm_

source=feedburner&utm_medium=feed&utm_campaign=Feed%3A+hechingerreport%2FphyU+%28Digital%29.
Kanter, M. J. (2011). American higher education: "First in the world." *Change: The Mazagine of Higher Learning*, May–June 2011. Retrieved on 13 June, 2013 from http://www.changemag.org/Archives/Back%20Issues/2011/May-June%202011/first-in-the-world-full.html.
Kehm, B. M. & Stensaker, B. (Eds.). (2009). *University rankings, diversity, and the new landscape of higher education*. Rotterdam: Sense Publishers.
Kelly, F. (2013). *Breakfast*. Australian Broadcasting Corporation, Radio National, 20 September, 2013.
Kemp, D. & Norton, A. (2014). *Review of the demand driven funding system report*. Canberra, ACT: Commonwealth of Australia.
Kendall, B. (2013). Advantage. *The Forum* with Katherine Asbury, Malcolm Gladwell & Ian Goldin. BBC World Service, 9 November, 2013. Retrieved on 10 November, 2013 from http://www.bbc.co.uk/iplayer/episode/p01ksh9h/The_Forum_Advantage/.
Kennedy, R. F. (1968). Speech made at the University of Kansas, 18 March, 1968. Retrieved on 21, 2014 from http://www.jfklibrary.org/Research/Research-Aids/Ready-Reference/RFK-Speeches/Remarks-of-Robert-F-Kennedy-at-the-University-of-Kansas-March-18-1968.aspx.
Kickert, W. (1995). Steering at a distance: A new paradigm of public governance in Dutch higher education. *Governance: An International Journal of Policy, Administration, and Institutions*, 8(1), 135–57.
Kitchen Garden Foundation (2014). Philosophy. Retrieved on 20 February, 2014 from http://www.kitchengardenfoundation.org.au/about-us/the-program/philosophy.
Klein, A. (2010). 18-to-24-year-olds most at risk for ID theft, survey finds. *Washington Post*, 17 March, 2010.
Knott, M. (2014). Education Minister Christoher Pyne: Set universities "free" to create a US-style system. *The Age*, 28 April, 2014.
Kohl, H. (2009). The educational panoptican. *Teachers College Record*, 8 January, 2009.
Konza, D. (2008). Inclusion of students with disabilities in new times: Responding to the challenge. In Kell, P., Vialle, W., Konza, D. & Vogl, G. (Eds.) *Learning and the learner: Exploring learning for new times*. Wollongong, NSW: University of Wollongong.
Kurzweil, R. (2005). *The singularity is near: When humans transcend biology*. New York: Viking Books.
Kynaston, D. (2013). Private schools are blocking social mobility. *The Telegraph*, 29 October, 2013.
Ladle, R. J., Malhado, A. C. M. & Todd, P. A. (2007). Access: Come all ye scientists, busy and exhausted. O come ye, O come ye, out of the lab. *Nature*, 450, 1156, 20 December, 2007.
Lebacqz, K. (1986). *Six theories of justice*. Minneapolis, MN: Augsburg Publishing House.
Lederman, D. (2013). CFO survey reveals doubts about financial sustainability. *Inside Higher Ed*, 12 July, 2013.
Lewin, T. (2013a). Students rush to web classes, but profits may be much later. *New York Times*, 6 January, 2013.
———. (2013b). Low-cost B.A. starting slowly in two states. *New York Times*, 18 October, 2013.
Loveless, T. (2006). *The 2006 Brown Center Report on American education: How well are American students learning?* Washington, DC: The Brookings Institution.
Lytton, M. (2011). Have all the costs of closing a school been considered? *CELE Exchange*. Centre for Effective Learning Environments, 2011, 1–4, 9–12.
MacBeath, J., Gray, J., Cullen, J., Frost, D., Steward, S. & Swaffield, S. (2007). *Schools on the Edge: Responding to Challenging Circumstances*. London: Paul Chapman Publishing.
Machin, S. & Silva, O. (2013). *School structure, school autonomy and the tail*. London: Centre for Economic Performance, London School of Economics and Political Science.
Mackay, H. (2013). *The good life: What makes life worth living?* South Yarra, Victoria: Pan Macmillan.

Madland, D. & Bunker, N. (2011). *Middle-class societies invest more in public education: A stronger middle class is associated with higher levels of spending on education.* Washington, DC: Center for American Progress.

Makin, P. J., Cooper, C. & Cox, C. J. (1996). *Organizations and the psychological contract.* Leicester, UK: British Psychological Society.

Mannheim, M. (2013). Public service stress claims soar. *The Sydney Morning Herald*, 29 July, 2013.

Marcoulides, G. A. & Heck, R. H. (1990). Educational policy issues for the 1990s: Balancing equity and excellence in implementing the reform agenda. *Urban Education*, 25(1), 55–67.

Marcus, J. & Koch, C. (2014). The future of brain implants. *The Australian*, 2 May, 2014, p. 18.

Marginson, M. (2010). How universities have been positioned as teams in a knowledge economy world cup. In Blackmore, J., Brennan, M. & Zipin, L. (Eds.) *Re-positioning university governance and academic work.* Rotterdam: Sense Publishers.

Marginson, S. (1993). *Education and public policy in Australia.* Melbourne, Victoria: Cambridge University Press.

———. (1997). *Markets in education.* St. Leonards, NSW: Allen & Unwin.

Marginson, S., Kaur, S. & Sawir, E. (2011). *Higher education in the Asia-Pacific. Strategic responses to globalization.* The Hague: Springer.

Marklein, M. B. (2012). Record number of foreign students in U. S. (2012). *USA Today*, 12 November, 2012.

Maslach, C. (1982). *Burnout: The cost of caring.* Englewood Cliffs, NJ: Prentice-Hall.

———. (1999). The truth about "burnout." *Life Matters*, Radio National, Australian Broadcasting Corporation, 14 April, 1999.

Maslen, G. (2013). Student poverty increasing by degrees. *The Age*, 22 July, 2013.

McLeod, B. (2014). $1tn Student debt crisis crushes home-buying dream. BBC News US & Canada, 11 April, 2014. Retrieved on 5 May, 2014 from http://www.bbc.com/news/world-us-canada-26893131

McNeil, L. M. (2000). *Contradictions of school reform: educational costs of standardized testing.* New York: Routledge.

Mencken, H. L. (1949). *A Mencken Chrestomathy.* New York: Alfred A. Knopf.

Meyer, W. (2011). The teacher salary myth—Are teachers underpaid? *Forbes Online*, 22 December, 2011. Retrieved on 25 February, 2014 from http://www.forbes.com/sites/warrenmeyer/2011/12/22/the-teacher-salary-myth-are-teachers-underpaid/.

Mickelburough, M. (2012). School shame as Victorian teachers quietly dismissed over misconduct including sexual abuse of students. *Herald Sun*, October 24, 2012.

Milburn, C. (2012). Why our best teachers are worth $150,000. *Sydney Morning Herald*, 21 May, 2012.

Miller Marsh, M. & Turner-Vorbeck, T. (Eds.) (2010). *(Mis)Understanding Families: Learning from real families in our schools.* New York: Teachers College Press.

Mitchell, C. (2013). Editorial, *The Age*, 23 October, 2013, 18.

Moore, G. E. (1965). Cramming more components onto integrated circuits. *Electronics*, 38 (8), April 19, 1965, 114–17.

Moore, P. (2014). Universal Pre-K: Wide support for expansion. YouGov, 10 March, 2014. Retrieved on 10 April, 2014 from http://today.yougov.com/news/2014/03/10/pre-k/.

Mozilla (2013). FAQ: Open badges. Retrieved on 29 August, 2013 from http://www.openbadges.org/faq/.

Napoli, N. (2013). *The school global budget and student resource package in Victoria: Twenty years of innovation and refinement.* Melbourne, Victoria: Financial Services Division, Department of Education and Early Childhood Development.

National Association of College and University Business Officers (NACUBO) (2013). NACUBO responds to White House college affordability plans, 14 November 2013. Retrieved on 12 December, 2013 from http://www.nacubo.org/Initiatives/Legislation_and_Congressional_Relations/Legislative_Updates/NACU-BO_Responds_to_White_House_College_Affordability_Plans.html.

New Zealand Government. (2012). *Delivering better public services: Boosting skills and employment by increasing education achievement for young people*. Wellington, NZ: Ministry of Education, New Zealand.

Ng, J. R. & Earl, J. K. (2008). Accuracy in self-assessment: The role of ability, feedback, self-efficacy and goal orientation. *Australian Journal of Career Development*, ACER, Spring 2008, 17(3), 39–50.

Noddings, N. (2003). *Happiness and education*. New York: Cambridge University Press.

Nous Group (2011). *Schooling challenges and opportunities*. Melbourne, Victoria: Nous Group.

O'Keefe, D. (Ed.) (1986). *The wayward curriculum: A cause for parents' concern*. Exeter, UK: Esmonde Publishing.

Organization for Economic Cooperation and Development (OECD) (2004). *Education at a glance 2004*. Paris: OECD.

Organization for Economic Cooperation and Development (OECD) (2007). *PISA 2006 Science competencies for tomorrow's world, Vol. 1*. Paris: OECD.

Organization for Economic Cooperation and Development (OECD) (2010a). *PISA 2009 Results: Overcoming social background, Volume 11*. Paris: OECD.

Organization for Economic Cooperation and Development (OECD) (2010b). *The high cost of low educational performance: the long-run economic impact of improving PISA outcomes*. Paris: OECD.

Organization for Economic Co-operation and Development (OECD). (2011a). Society: Governments must tackle record gap between rich and poor says OECD. Retrieved on 5 December, 2013 from http://www.oecd.org/newsroom/societygovernmentsmusttackle recordgapbetweenrichandpoorsaysoecd.htm.

Organisation for Economic Co-operation and Development (OECD). (2011b). Divided we stand: Why inequality keeps rising. Paris: OECD. Retrieved on 5 December 2013 from http://www.oecd.org/social/soc/dividedwestandwhyinequalitykeepsrising.htm.

Organization for Economic Cooperation and Development (OECD) (2012). *PISA 2012: assessment and analytical framework*. Paris: OECD.

Organization for Economic Cooperation and Development (OECD) (2013). *Education at a glance 2013: OECD indicators*. Paris: OECD.

Orwell, G. (1949). *Nineteen Eighty-Four. A novel*. London, UK: Secker & Warburg.

Orwell, G. (1965). *Animal farm: A fairy story*. Harmondsworth, Middlesex: Penguin.

Owens, J. D. & Price, L. (2010). Is e-learning replacing the traditional lecture? *Education & Training*, 52(2), 128–39.

Parrish, T. B. & Wolman, J. (2004). How is special education funded? Issues and implications for school administrators. *NASSP Bulletin*, 88(640), 57–68.

Paton, G. (2010). Student debts "to reach 25,000 pounds." *The Telegraph*, 13 August, 2013.

Petre, J. (2013). Colleges hit by grade inflation row as EVERYONE gets a top degree on dozens of university courses. *Mail Online*, 12 October, 2013. Accessed on 14 October, 2013 from http://www.dailymail.co.uk/news/article-2456254/Dozens-British-degree-courses-single-student-getting-grades.html.

Piety, P. (2013). *Assessing the educational data movement*. New York: Teachers College Press.

Polesel, J., Dulfer, N. & Turnbull, M. (2012). *The experience of education: The impacts of high stakes testing on school students and their families*. Rydalmere, NSW: Whitlam Institute within the University of Western Sydney.

Postman, N. (1995). *The end of education*. New York: Vintage Books.

Postman, N. & Weingartner, C. (1969). *Teaching as a subversive activity*. Guildford, UK: Delta Publishing.

Power, M. (1997). *The audit society: Rituals or verification*. Oxford: Oxford University Press.

———. (1999). *The audit implosion: Regulating risk from the inside*. London: ICAEW.

Preiss, B. (2012). Positive thinking centre on campus. *The Age*, 3 April, 2012.

———. (2012a). Queries on school finance reporting. *The Age*, 23 October, 2012.

———. (2013a). Student achievement levels slip. *The Age*, 16 August, 2013.

———. (2013b). Shake-up to hit state school principals. *The Saturday Age*, 28 September, 2013, p. 1.

Preston, B. (2013). *The social make-up of schools: Family income, Indigenous status, family type, religion and broadband access of students in government, Catholic and other non-government schools.* A Report conducted for the Australian Education Union by Barbara Preston Research, April 2013. O'Connor, ACT: Barbara Preston Research.
Productivity Commission (2013). *Productivity Update, May 2013.* Canberra, ACT: Productivity Commission, Australian Government.
Prunty, J. (1985). Signposts for a critical educational policy analysis. *Australian Journal of Education*, 29(2), 133–40.
———. (1987). *A critical reformulation of educational policy analysis*, 2nd ed. Geelong, Victoria: Deakin University Press.
Pryor, L. (2008). *The pinstriped prison: How overachievers get trapped in the corporate jobs they hate.* Sydney, NSW: Picador.
Quenemoen, R. F., Lehr, C. A., Thurlow, M. L. & Massanari, C. B. (2001). *Students with disabilities in standards-based assessment and accountability systems: Emerging issues, strategies, and recommendations. Synthesis Report 37.* Minneapolis, MN: National Center on Educational Outcomes, University of Minnesota.
Quiggin, J. (2011). *Zombie economics: How dead ideas still walk among us.* Princeton, NJ: Princeton University Press.
Raab, C. (1994). Theorising the governance of education. *British Journal of Educational Studies*, 42(1), 6–22.
Ravitch, D. (2010). *The death and life of the great American school system: How testing and choice are undermining education.* New York: Basic Books.
Rawls, J. (1972). *A theory of justice.* Oxford: Oxford University Press.
Rees, M. (2003). *Our final hour. A scientist's warning: How terror, error, and environmental disaster threaten humankind's future in this century—on earth and beyond.* New York: Basic Books.
Reid, A. (2005). Rethinking the democratic purposes of public schooling in a globalising world. In Apple, M., Kenway, J. & Singh, M. (Eds.) *Globalizing education: policies, pedagogies and politics.* New York: Peter Lang.
———. (2009). Is this really a revolution? A critical analysis of the Rudd government's national education agenda. *Curriculum Perspectives*, 9(3): 1–13.
———. (2012). A dumbed down debate, but those tests still hold some lessons.*Sydney Morning Herald*, 19 December, 2012.
———. (2013). Quality of teaching and learning should be key priorities for public education. *The Advertiser*, 12 August, 2013.
Reivich, K., Gillham, J. E., Chaplin, T. M. & Seligman, M. E. P. (2005). From helplessness to optimism. The role of resilience in treating and preventing depression in youth. In Goldstein, S. & Brooks, R. B. (Eds.) *Handbook of resilience in children.* New York: S. Kluwer Academic/Plenum Publishers.
Reuchlin, M. (1972). *Individual orientation in education.* The Hague: Springer.
Richards, E. (2014). Bill would close failing Wisconsin public schools, cut voucher payments. *Milwaukee Journal Sentinel*, 28 January, 2014.
Robinson, K. (2010). Bring on the learning revolution! TED talk filmed February 2010 at TED 2010. Retrieved on 1 May, 2013 from www.ted.com/talks/sir_ken_robinson_bring_on_the_revolution.
Sadurski, W. (1985). *Giving desert its due: Social justice and legal theory.* Dordrecht, The Netherlands: Kluwer Press (Reidal).
Sandel, M. J. (2012). *What money can't buy: The moral limits of markets.* London: Penguin.
Savage, G. C. (2014). Why markets can't deliver excellence and equity in schools. The Conversation, 8 May, 2014. Retrieved 12 May 2014 from http://theconversation.com/why-markets-cant-deliver-excellence-and-equity-in-schools-25711.
Schaufeldi, W., Maslach, C. & Tadeusz, M. (Eds.). (1996). *Professional burnout: Recent developments in theory and research.* Washington, DC: Taylor & Francis.
Schiller, B. (2013). 8 new jobs people will have in 2025. Fast Company, 15 August, 2013. Retrieved on 21 August, 2013 from http://www.fastcoexist.com/3015652/futurist-forum/8-new-jobs-people-will-have-in-2025.

Schneider, J. (2011). *Excellence for all: How a new breed of reformers is transforming America's public schools*. Nashville, TN: Vanderbilt University Press.

Schor, J. B. (1992). *The overworked American: The unexpected decline of leisure*. New York: Basic Books.

Shore, C. & Roberts, S. (1993). Higher education and the Panoptican paradigm: Quality assessment as "disciplinary technology." Paper presented at the Society for Research into Higher Education conference "Governments and the higher education curriculum: Evolving partnerships," University of Sussex, England, 14–16 December, 1993.

Simon, S. (2013). U.S. spends big on education, but results lag many nations: OECD. *Reuters*, 25 June, 2013. Retrieved on 25 June, 2013 from http://www.reuters.com/article/2013/06/25/us-usa-education-oecd-idUSBRE95O0CN20130625.

Simos, M. (2013). Red tape makes us too tired to teach. *Adelaide Now*, 26 March, 2013. Retrieved on 25 February, 2014 from http://www.adelaidenow.com.au/news/south-australia/new-government-policies-create-massive-tiring-workload-for-preschool-directors-childcare-workers-and-teachers/story-e6frea83-.

Sloan, J. (2014). Studied lessons in career suicide. *The Australian*, 15 February, 2014.

Smith, A. (1776). *The wealth of nations, Vols. 1 & 2*. London: Strahan & Cadell.

———. (1869). *The theory of moral sentiments,* 2nd edition. London: Bell & Daldy.

———. (2014). Rich families should have to pay to attend public schools, report says. *Sydney Morning Herald*, 20 April, 2014.

Smyth, J. (Ed.) (1993). *A socially critical view of the "self-managing school."* Bristol, UK: The Falmer Press.

Smyth, J. & Shacklock, G. (2004). Teachers doing their "economic" work. In S. J. Ball (Ed.). *The RoutledgeFalmer Reader in Sociology of Education*. London: RoutledgeFalmer, 240–56.

Starr, K. (1991). Justice for whom? A critique of the social justice strategy of the South Australian Education Department. *South Australian Educational Leader*, 2(5), December 1991, Adelaide, SA: The Centre for Students in Educational Leadership, University of South Australia.

Starr, K. E. (1999). That roar which lies on the other side of silence: An analysis of women principals' responses to structural reform in South Australian education. Adelaide, South Australia: Unpublished PhD thesis, Library of University of South Australia.

Starr, K. (2007). *Principal "Disengagement": Are the Solutions Addressing the Problem?* In Donahoo, S. & Hunter, R. C. (Eds.) *Teaching Leaders to Lead Teachers: Educational Administration in the Era of Constant Change*. Oxford: Elsevier Science, 335–53.

Starr, K. (2009). Pressing Issues in the New Context of Australian Educational Leadership. In Ehrich, L. & Cranston, N. (Eds.) *Australian Educational Leadership Today: Issues and Trends*. Brisbane, Queensland: Social Science Press, 21–38.

———. (2011a). Doing justice: Contemplating language and equity. In *The Australian Educational Leaders, Official Journal of the Australian Council of Educational Leaders*, 33(1), 22–24.

———. (2011b). Principals and the politics of resistance to change. *Educational Management, Administration and Leadership*: 39(6): 646–60.

———. (2012a). Problematizing risk and the principalship: The risky business of managing risk in schools. *Educational Management, Administration and Leadership*, 40(4), 464–79.

———. (2012b). *Above and Beyond the Bottom Line: The extraordinary evolution of education business management*. Camberwell, Victoria: ACER Press.

———. (2012c). Refining pedagogy by reviewing professional learning for online course delivery. In Peterson, J.; Lee, O.; Islam, T. & Piscioneri, M. (Eds.) *Effectively implementing information communication technology in higher education in the Asia-Pacific Region*. Hauppage, NY: Nova Science, 221–34.

———. (2013a). All take and no give? Support and development needs of women in part-time and casual academic roles. In Beaton, F. and Gilbert, A. (Eds.) *Effective part-time teachers in contemporary universities: new approaches to professional development*. London: Routledge.

———. (2013b). The increasing importance and imperative of the school business manager. In *School Business Affairs*, 79(3), 21–24.

———. (2014a). The influences and implications of PISA: An Australian perspective. *AASA Journal of Scholarship & Practice*, Winter 2014, 10(4), 19–29.

———. (2014b). Interrogating conceptions of leadership: school principals, policy and paradox. *School leadership & Management*, Taylor & Francis: Published online 16 April, 2014. Retrieved 5 May, 2014 from http://www.tandfonline.com/doi/full/10.1080/13632434.2014.905466#.U3FHo8dilxM.

Starr, K. & Toffoletti, K. (2010). *Enhancing Deakin University's Status as an Employer of Choice for Women*. Waurn Ponds, Victoria: Knowledge Media Division, Deakin University.

Starr, K., Stacey, E. & Grace, L. (2011). Changing Technologies/Renewing Pedagogies: Implications for University Teaching and Learning. In Trentin, G. & Repetto, M. (Eds.) *Faculty Training on Web Enhanced Learning*. Hauppauge, NY: Nova Science Publishers, 95–108.

Stiglitz, J. E. (2012). *The price of inequality*. London: Allen Lane.

Sustainability Victoria (2014). *Schools*. Retrieved on 20 February, 2014 from http://www.sustainability.vic.gov.au/Services-and-Advice/Schools.

Suzuki, D. (2013). Interview on Q&A, Australian Broadcasting Corporation, 23 September, 2013.

Sweet, R. (2013). Not earning or learning. *Life Matters*, Australian Broadcasting Corporation, Radio National, 4 November, 2013. Retrieved on 5 November, 2013 from http://www.abc.net.au/radionational/programs/lifematters/not-earning-or-learning/5065070.

Tapscott, D. (2012). Discovery learning is the new higher learning. *The Globe and Mail*, 15 October, 2012. Retrieved on 29 August, 2013 from http://www.theglobeandmail.com/commentary/discovery-learning-is-the-new-higher-learning/article4610656/.

Teese, R. (with assistance from Walstab, A.). (2011). *From opportunity to outcomes. The changing role of public schooling in Australian and national funding arrangements*. Carlton, Victoria: Centre for Research on Education Systems, Melbourne Graduate School of Education, University of Melbourne.

Teese, R., Nicholas, T., Polesel, J. & Helme, S. (2005). *The Destinations of School Leavers in Victoria: A Report of the 2005 On Track Project*. Melbourne: Centre for Post-compulsory Education and Lifelong Learning, University of Melbourne.

Teichler, U. (2009). Between over-diversification and over-homogenization: Five decades of search for a creative fabric of higher education. In Kehm, B. M. & Stensaker, B. (Eds.). (2009). *University rankings, diversity, and the new landscape of higher education*. Rotterdam: Sense Publishers.

The Age (2010). Hard lessons for better leadership. *The Age*, 4 September, 2010.

The Australian (2013). School funding must lift results. Opinion, *The Australian*, 3 December, 2013.

The Economist (2010a). Learning the right lessons. *The Economist*, 9 September. 2010.

The Economist (2013a). Catching on at last: New technology is poised to disrupt America's schools, and then the world's. *The Economist*, 29 June, 2013.

The Economist (2013b). Get them while they're young. *The Economist*, 408(8850), 24–30 August, 2013.

The Economist (2013c). Get a life. *The Economist*, 24 September, 2013.

Thomson, S., Hillman, K. & De Bortoli, L. (2013a). *A teacher's guide to PISA reading literacy*. Camberwell, Victoria: ACER Press.

———. (2013b). *A teacher's guide to PISA mathematical literacy*. Camberwell, Victoria: ACER Press.

Tickle, L. (2012). Academy status: Is a head's job secure when a school is forced to switch? *The Guardian*, 21 September, 2012.

Tienken, C. H. (2014). PISA problems. *AASA Journal of Scholarship & Practice*, 10(4), Winter 2014, 4–18.

Tingle, L. (2014). Hockey spells out the detail behind "budget crisis." *Financial Review*, 23 April, 2014.

Toffler, A. (1970). *Future Shock*. New York: Random House.

Tomazin, F. (2012). School staff in rort scandal. *The Age*, 29 January, 2012.

Topsfield, J. (2012a). The Mowbray Way. *The Age*, 9 June, 2012, 15.
———. (2012b). No cheer for Mowbray creditors. *The Age*, 9 June, 2012.
———. (2012c). MLC principal in shock after sacking over money. *The Age*, 19 September, 2012.
———. (2012d). MLC parents demand board reinstate sacked principal. *The Age*, 28 September, 2012.
———. (2012e). Schools built on sand. *The Age*, 28 October, 2012.
———. (2012f). Schools found cheating on national tests. *The Age*, 18 January, 2012.
———. (2012g). Aboriginal schools fail to deliver. *The Age*, 26 June, 2012.
———. (2013a). Going it alone. *The Age*, 12 August, 2013.
Tovey, J. (2013). Bigger classes free teachers to raise standards. *Sydney Morning Herald*, 2 March, 2013.
Trainor, M. F. (2012). *About Earth's child: An ecological listening to the Gospel of Luke*. Sheffield, UK: Sheffield Phoenix Press.
Twigg, S. (2013). Profit-making schools will bring chaos and cut standards. *The Independent*, 3 July, 2013. Retrieved on 6 December, 2013 from http://www.independent.co.uk/voices/comment/profit-making-schools-will-bring-chaos-and-cut-standards-8683763.html.
Tytherleigh, M. Y., Webb, C., Cooper, C. L. & Ricketts, C. (2005). Occupational stress in UK higher education institutions: A comparative study of all staff categories. *Higher Education Research & Development*, 24(1), 41–61.
UNESCO (United Nations Educational Scientific and Cultural Organization) (1997). *Educating for a sustainable future*. Paris: UNESCO.
UNESCO (2007). *The UN decade of education for sustainable development (DESD 2005–2014): The first two years*. Paris: UNESCO.
UNESCO (2012). *Youth research: Education and skills. International qualitative research for the 2012 Education for All Global Monitoring Report—Youth and skills: Putting education to work*. London: GLobeScan.
University of Sydney (2011). *Policies Development and Review Rule 2011*. Retrieved on 29 July, 2013 from http://sydney.edu.au/legal/policy/what/index.shtml
USAction Education Fund (2011). *Hardly working: Stories from under-employed Americans*. Washington, DC: USAction Education Fund.
U.S. Department of Education (2014). *College affordability and transparency center*. Retrieved 24 April, 2014 from www.collegecost.ed.gov.
Vaizey, J. (1962). *The economics of education*. London: Faber & Faber.
Van der Doef, M. & Maes, S. (1999). The job demand-control (-support) model and psychological well-being: A review of 20 years of empirical research. *Work and Stress*, 13(2), 87–114.
Van Nieuwerburgh, C. (2012). *Coaching in education: Getting better results for students, educators and parents*. Professional Coaching Series. London: Karnac Books.
Vedder, R., Denhart, C. & Robe, J. (2013). *Why are recent college graduates unemployed?* Washington, DC: Center for College Affordability and Productivity, January 2013.
Victorian Auditor-General. (2012). *Obsolescence of frontline ICT: Police and schools*. Victorian Government Printer, PP No 142, Session 2010–12.
Wagenaar, R. (2008). *Learning outcomes a fair way to measure performance in higher education: The TUNING approach*. Paris: OECD.
Wagner, R. B. (1989). *Accountability in education: A philosophical inquiry*. New York: Routledge.
Walker, S. J. (2013). UK higher education: Let's not follow the leaders but develop our own vision. *The Guardian, Higher Education Network*, 21 May, 2013.
Webb, P. T., Briscoe, F. M. & Mussmann, M. P. (2009). Preparing teachers for the neoliberal Panoptican. *Educational Foundations*, Summer-Fall 2009, 23(3–4), 3–18.
Wellman, J. V. (2008). The higher education funding disconnect: Spending more, getting less. *Change: The magazine of higher learning*. November–December 2008.
White, J. (2012). Scholarly identity. In Fitzgerald, T., White, J. & Gunter, H. M. (2012). *Hard labour? Academic work and the changing landscape of higher education*. Bingley, UK: Emerald Group Publishing.

Wolnizer, P. W. (1987). *Auditing as independent authentication.* Sydney, NSW: Sydney University Press.

Wong, K. K. & Shen, F. X. (2013). *Mayoral governance and student achievement: How mayor-led districts are improving school and student performance.* March 2013. Washington, DC: Center for American Progress.

Wren, B. (1986). *Education for justice.* 2nd edition. London: SCM Press.

Wright, P. (2013). Why new technologies could never replace great teaching. *The Guardian*, 21 June, 2013.

Wright, T. & Horst, N. (2013). Exploring the ambiguity: What faculty leaders really think of sustainability in higher education. *International Journal of Sustainability in Higher Education*, 14(2), 209–27.

Wuorio, J. (2012). Startups take on the business of education. *Entrepreneur*, 8 October, 2012. Retrieved on 6 December, 2013 from http://www.entrepreneur.com/article/224565.

Young, S. (2013). Private schools and the art of ripping off parents. *The Age*, 4 September, 2013.

Zeehandelaar, D. & Northern, A. M. (2013). *What parents want: Educational preferences and trade-offs.* Thomas B. Fordham Institute.

Zeichner, K. & Pena-Sandoval, C. (2015). Venture philanthropy and teachers education policy in the U.S.: The role of the New Schools Venture Fund. *Teachers College Record*, 117(6), 2015.

Zencey, E. (2009). GDP RIP. *New York Times*, 9 August, 2009.

Zyngier, D. (2011). Education funding: more dollars than sense. *The Conversation*, 3 September 2013. Retrieved on 11 November, 2013 from http://theconversation.com/education-funding-more-dollars-than-sense-2934

www.ingramcontent.com/pod-product-compliance
Lightning Source LLC
Chambersburg PA
CBHW052130300426
44116CB00010B/1851